Raising A Family

Raising
A Family

Living on Planet Parenthood

Jeanne Elium
Don Elium

Celestial Arts Publishing
Berkeley, California

We are extremely grateful to our clients, colleagues, friends, and families who shared personal accounts of their lives with us. To protect their privacy, names, anecdotes, and case histories have been changed and, in many cases, woven together.

Celestial Arts Publishing
P.O. Box 7123
Berkeley, CA 94707

"There's a Hole in My Sidewalk" is reproduced with the gracious permission of Beyond Words Publishing:

© 1993 Portia Nelson
From the book *There's a Hole in My Sidewalk*
Beyond Words Publishing, Inc.
4443 NE Airport Road, Hillsboro, OR 97124, 1(800)284-9673

Cover design by Design Site
Text design by Victor Ichioka
Typesetting by Greene Design
Printed in the United States

Library of Congress Cataloging-in-Publication Data

Elium, Jeanne, 1947–
    Raising a family : living on planet parenthood / Jeanne Elium,
Don Elium.
        p.   cm.
    Includes index.
    ISBN 0-89087-818-8
    1. Family. 2. Marriage. 3. Parenting. I. Elium, Don, 1954– .
II. Title.
HQ734.E42   1997
306.85—dc21   .   97–5375
                                                      CIP

1 2 3 4 5 6 – 00 99 98 97

In great appreciation
we lovingly dedicate this book
to
Landry Wildwind

ACKNOWLEDGMENTS

A graduate student at John F. Kennedy University, Orinda, California, once handed us a barely readable, xeroxed piece of paper with a poem called, "Autobiography in Five Short Chapters." No author was mentioned. The poem was so moving and such a profound description of how change happens, Don began to structure his psychology classes around it. For years we tried to locate the author to thank him or her. Through a set of strange coincidences, one of our publishers put us in contact with actress, lyricist, composer, and writer, Portia Nelson, the author of this amazing poem. Portia's poem and indomitable spirit guides our souls in bringing new life to our family and others by her gracious consent to let us put her poem to work in the heart of our writing about family life. She so beautifully teaches us to walk away from the paths of habit down a different street that welcomes our souls' desires. Thank you, Portia, from all our hearts. And many thanks to Beyond Words Publishing for their gracious permission to use Portia's poem.

We also have much gratitude for our agent, Peter Beren, all the folks at Celestial Arts, especially David Hinds and Veronica Randall, all of the participants in our audiences and workshops, our clients, our friends, our children Matthew and Heidi, and family for their honest feedback, loving support, and enduring patience. We love you all.

CONTENTS

Authors' Preface

◁※▷ *JEANNE* I wrote this book to learn to let go. I come from tough pioneer stock who believed that life is work, and after the work is done, then you can have fun. Maybe. If there is time left over, and if no other work presents itself; which it probably will. It usually does. I am very good at finding more work to be done; I have not been very good at relaxing or having fun. As I get older, I realize I may have missed out on something.

Although I am a retired elementary school teacher, government employee, community service agency director, personnel trainer, and women's counselor, and currently lead workshops, speak professionally, co-host a radio show, co-write a column, author books, and mother a nine-year-old, the bulk of my work has been home upkeep and management—cooking, cleaning, washing, clearing, straightening, repairing, and planning. I am sure someone has calculated how many hours during her lifetime a woman spends doing housework, but even if she is a mother-at-home, it is far too many. I say "even if she is a mother-at-home," because they are expected to do the housework, right? Well, I believe mothering and home management are each full-time jobs, and if fathers want to belong in the family, they must assume an equitable share of the home care, whether Mom works outside it or not.

With that off my chest, I now confess I have difficulty sharing. I like things done just a certain way at home—how the towels are folded and put away, how the dishwasher is loaded, and how the groceries are stored. I like knowing I will find the salad spinner in the same place each time I want to use it. Routine and order bring calm to my otherwise hectic world. When I share these routine tasks with a man and a nine-year-old boy, I lose control. And, if I share the responsibility of planning for the family (a much bigger role than doing routine tasks)—menus, grocery lists, scheduling and keeping appointments, making social engagements and following through on them, keeping everyone in haircuts, dental check-ups, and clothes and shoes that fit, recycling, paying bills, being neighborly, monitoring the upkeep of the car, house, and yard, and either doing the repairs or arranging to have them done—how can I trust it will all get done and my way???

By this time, many of you reading this are probably thinking, "This woman is nuts! Who would want to do all that work when they don't have to?" However, in my conversations over the years with many, many women on this very subject, we agree that no matter how overburdened we are, it is hard to share the power at home with a man. And that is what this difficulty is about—Power. And Safety.

I am extremely grateful when someone else mops the kitchen floor, does a load of laundry, or goes grocery shopping, but it is much harder for me to give up my super-vigilant thinking, planning, and considering of the family. I call it my "Mother Hen" habit. I keep my family and our home safe and together under gigantic, invisible, motherly wings. Thinking I have to do this alone makes the responsibility seem overwhelming—and lonely.

How do I describe what I just naturally do as a mother and homemaker? How do I learn to share the responsibility and power? How do I let go into a more trusting and equitable relationship with my parenting partner? How do I find more space in the kitchen?

⊷ ⊷ *DON*I wrote this book to discover how to live and belong in the emotional core of my family while retaining my uniqueness as a man. These key questions kept popping up from within myself and from my clients: Why are women and children acknowledged as a family unit with Dad often left on the outside? Why, when a man prepares five out of seven family dinners, is he described as "helping out around the house?" Why, when a woman works full-time, is she said to be "helping out with the finances?" Why, no matter how hard he tries, is a man criticized for never doing enough, being like a "bull in a china closet," and just not being there? Why, when women say they need help with the physical and emotional demands of child rearing and home care, do men feel they never do enough and are left on the edges of family life? Why do men seem to be shut out of family life and women, locked into it, whether they are good at the job, or whether they like it or not?

In writing this book, I sought to find how men and women can truly be partners in home and child care while maintaining their unique gender differences and gifts. Acknowledging and respecting the differences between women and men was helpful but not enough of a solution. I realized I had to change. I had to admit there was something here that I did not know. How could I expand my thinking and being in the domestic world where I have no training, biological instinct, or cultural support? How do I function in a family without betraying my masculine heritage, without learning to do and think just like my wife? The answers, it seems, lie outside my masculine hardwiring, in the latent cells just waiting to be awakened, the softwiring of the male brain.

I invite the men who read this book to join me in changing what no other men in recorded history have had to change. These changes do not require giving up our manhood. We are being called to expand our manhood to meet the spiritual, emotional, and physical needs of children at home. In this expansion process, we learn to share the leadership of home and child care, becoming partners with our spouses and belonging in our families. Children desperately need dads to really be home.

PART ONE

Welcome to Planet Parenthood

Before I got married
I had six theories about bringing up children;
now I have six children,
and no theories.

—Lord Rochester

Life before children. Do any of us remember what that was like? Staying up late; sleeping in; sleeping the whole night through without getting up to walk the baby, rock the baby, change the baby, or feed the baby; going out to dinner, dancing, and a movie on a whim without planning ahead; having a complete conversation, uninterrupted by, "Mommeee, Daddeee, look at meeeee," every two seconds; spending at least two hours in a row on a project; finding everything on the desk in the same place we left it yesterday; taking a bath without a rubber ducky, a Power Ranger figure, or a Barbie doll floating to the surface between our legs; leaving the house unencumbered by a diaper bag, stroller, snacks, bottles, blankie, infant seat, backpack carrier, and toys; running more than one errand *quickly* in one car trip; getting past the checkout line without several silly items our child could not live without; settling onto the couch for an intimate snuggle without a little head popping up between us; using the car for errands, transportation to work, or pleasure, rather than as a taxi service; getting to use the car when we want to; not having to deal with nose rings, telephone rings, and smoke rings; making chocolate mousse instead of chocolate m & m cookies; experiencing complete silence in the house, in the car, anywhere!!!!!

Let's face it: kids change our sleeping habits, our waistlines, our pocketbooks, our sex lives, our long-range plans, our short-range plans, and, most of all, the way we *have* to think. Men may be from Mars, and women may be from Venus, but kids take us to a different galaxy. Welcome to Planet Parenthood!

Here is what some of the inhabitants of this new planet have to say:

"Mostly, I miss the freedom to do what I want, when I want."

"It's like being in love all over again, only different."

"Spontaneity just flies out the window."

"Having kids added more stress to our lives."

"I had to grow up myself."

"We got jealous of the time we each spent with the baby."

"Our friends changed. Those without kids excluded us and eventually there was nothing to talk about anymore."

"Having kids gave us a new feeling of responsibility to be more introspective about our behavior: How does what we do affect them; what messages does our behavior convey to them?"

"When the babies came, my husband just worked harder."

"Our relationship deepened after we had children. We had to meet the challenge of staying in touch and in love in spite of all the distractions, exhaustion, work, and money worries."

"We now make friends in different social settings: play groups, the sandlot at the park, PTA, swim team practices, soccer games, or school dances."

"Our marriage seemed to break apart after we had kids. We just didn't have time to do anything together, and everything was a big hassle between us."

"I love being a mom. I wish it paid better!"

"My wife focuses more on what everybody else needs than on what I need."

"I can no longer think only for myself. I have to think for everyone else. It's exhausting!"

"The more I work at my job and home, the less my wife appreciates me."

"As a single parent, I work my buns off for my children and make sure they have what they need—they are my life. I won't let happen to them what happened to me!"

We all come to parenthood differently. Some of us carefully plan until the time is right to have a child; many of us blunder into parenthood; others of us try and try, eventually adopting the hoped-for little one. However it happens, no one can prepare us for the inevitable changes having children brings to every moment of our lives. Suddenly we are catapulted onto a different planet. On this planet, we find interests we never knew we had. It is not unusual to have long conversations about the color of baby poop, spit up, purple hair, and body piercing. Everyday situations take on new meaning; what was commonplace or taken-for-granted before now presents new risks and challenges. Wall sockets, lamp cords, and stairs become threatening; the neighbors drive too fast down our street; our old, beloved dog is jealous of the baby; no longer can we leave hammers and saws lying around that unfinished project. We become more critical of television and advertising. We are more concerned about the quality of our local elementary school, the air we breathe, the water we drink. Perhaps for the first time we look to the future and consider how our lifestyles affect the world we are bequeathing to our children and grandchildren.

Often, this natural concern for our children's welfare takes us back into our own childhoods, searching for clues about how we were parented, what was positive and what was not. We examine our relationships with our parents and wonder whether we want the same with our children. Our own parenthood offers many of us a chance to redeem or transform the bonds we had with our parents, knowing we must resolve old grievances before we can get on with the task of parenting our children.

No longer do we merely think for and about ourselves and our mates. Our first thoughts in the morning and our last thoughts at night are about our children—what they did, how they are, what didn't get done for them, what must be done tomorrow, how much we love them, how to keep them safe.

But, Where Are the Instructions?

When we bring home a new gadget, one of the first things we pull out of the box (and often the last thing we read) are instructions for how to put it together and how to turn it on. If pieces are missing or the blankety-blank thing doesn't work, we can call a 24-hour, toll-free number to find out exactly how to fix it. If all else fails, we can send it back to the manufacturer who will send us a NEW one, free of charge, that does what it is supposed to do!

The situation is very different, however, when a new child comes into our lives. There are no "operating instructions!" Rather than directions, the paperwork involves insurance forms, hospital bills, and payment schedules. We can buy helpful advice from parenting books, but there are no individualized instructions for this new being, no toll-free numbers, no return labels enclosed. On Planet Parenthood, we take what comes, and the exhilarating, exasperating adventure into this new world begins.

Although parents do have access to excellent, practical parenting advice, such as how to bathe, diaper, feed, and understand the baby, the true mission, real identity, and genuine needs of this new being are not to be found in a book or learned from an expert. This vital information is stored inside our little one in a special place that, like a seed, has its own time-table of development. Parenting is an adventure, and a child is a mystery with a unique purpose that unfolds one step at a time.

When children first come into our lives, the joy, excitement, and newness of it all soothe our exhaustion, cover our feelings of inadequacy, and mask our fears. We are carried along on a euphoric high. After we adjust to the required new rhythms, we may be surprised by the dramatic changes parenthood brings. Single friends and couples without kids drop out of our lives. Sleep becomes a priceless luxury. Laundry becomes a formidable mountain. Like it or not, we become members of a different group of people. We feel it more deeply as time goes on, and we become more aware of feeling cut off from old friends, our parents, our partners, our own selves. In the beginning, we attribute these reactions to the new baby and the new responsibilities of parenthood. It is often not until our youngest child is three or four that we finally acknowledge something has irreversibly changed. Our life is not getting back to the "normal" that we unconsciously defined as, "life before the kids came." Our marriage feels the strain, our personal fulfillment is on hold, and we can see no farther than the next meal or the trail of toys from the kitchen to every other room in the house. We feel overwhelmed by all the needs and at a loss over what to do about them. "There's never enough time!" becomes our constant lament.

This mild complaint carries greater significance than we may understand at first glance. Beneath the surface of, "There's never enough time," lies an unspoken discontent, frustration, and even anguish about life on Planet Parenthood. This phrase reveals the loneliness, confusion, and hurt that often exists in today's families. "There's never enough time" is translated differently by different people. Fathers may mean:

"I no longer have any male friends."

"I now work more on the job *and* at home and feel unappreciated in both places."

"No one can even see the pain and sacrifices I make daily."

"I can never seem to do enough to please my mate or my children."

"Our sex life? What sex life?"

"I don't feel I belong in my own family. That's why I work all the time. At least there I get a positive response."

"She gives a telemarketer more respect, care, and information about her life than she gives to me."

By "There's never enough time," mothers often mean:

"Now I have to think for everybody. My spouse acts like another kid."

"No one cares about what I need."

"I have two full-time jobs—one at work and one at home."

"I am tired of describing myself as a 'mom-working-at-home.' What's wrong with MOTHER? No one seems to value my full-time parenting and the second job that gets tossed in there, the house-keeper!"

"I feel exhausted, angry, and depressed most of the time."

"I miss sex, but after a long day, sex is the last thing on my mind."

For single parents, "There's never enough time" involves many other issues:

"I am alone with so many responsibilities."

"My ex-spouse changes from friend to adversary over the smallest of details!"

"I don't think I will ever catch up."

"Dating is a hassle at my age and with children."

"When someone hears I'm a single parent, I can tell they're thinking, 'One parent can't raise good kids.'"

"What's a sex life?"

"There's never enough time," really means that something is not right; something is missing from our lives. We are trying to describe a crucial phenomenon, but we don't know its name. The harder we try, the more elusive it gets, and the more we want to blame it on something outside of ourselves: "If only we were out of debt." "If only the kids were older." "If only I had married the other guy/girl." We seem faced with two alternatives—to grit our teeth and carry on in quiet desperation, hoping that "winning the lottery" will save us, or to be caught up in a constant struggle with our family members as we face the never-ending horizon of unmet needs.

Looking for Family-making in All the Wrong Places

> *"Why is it, that the more I read, learn, and improve my parenting skills, the worse my relationship with my spouse is, the less I know my own needs, and the more lonely I become?"*
> *—Janet, mother of three*

≪ ≪ Don | So often in couple's therapy, parents report that their family is a wreck, that their relationship is dried up, and they are overwhelmed by the unmet needs. The interesting thing is that these parents are usually intensely focused on and doing a good job of raising their children. Parenting has consumed them to such an extent that there is little energy or motivation left to nurture the couple relationship. Parenting a child, making money, and keeping house have replaced the concept of raising a family.

To most of us, the definition of *family* is a verb rather than a noun meaning: "to raise children." With parenting information so well developed and presented in the many workshops and books available on the subject, our focus is skewed to see only the needs of the children. The other elements of a family become lost in parenting concerns, and it seems that the more expert we are, the harder it is to have a healthy family life. Thus, mates complain that they feel unseen, unheard, uncared for, and that they no longer belong in their families.

The big mistake most of us make is to try to solve the problem of FAMILY by becoming better parents or by improving ourselves through individual therapy. More insight about parenting and our own inner selves is always beneficial, but this information in itself will not make healthier families. **Being good parents does not necessarily make our families work better.** Improving our parenting skills may further separate us from our own needs, our mate's needs, and the needs of our family group. Using the language of good parenting, self-help psychology, or couple's therapy falls short when we want to have a family that works. Although much research on families has been conducted, there is little written information describing the principles of family-making and how to live together as a group. Using therapy or self-help books that focus on how to function as an individual or as a couple simply does not translate into family-making that includes childrearing. When children arrive, we lose our awareness of our coupleness and grouphood.

The solution, therefore, is to shift our focus from childrearing language to a family-making language that INCLUDES parenting, as well as couple life, individual life, and group life. When we define *family* as a noun—"a group of related people"—this broader interpretation can include not only the parenting of children, but the nurturing of the relationships between group members as well. Raising a family becomes relationship-focused—between Mom and Dad, between Mom and child/ren, between Dad and child/ren, between sibling and sibling. This book is our effort to develop a family-making language and a way of thinking that makes families thrive and survive on Planet Parenthood.

PART TWO

You Can't Mix
Apples and Oranges

*Until you make the problem clear
there's no way you're going
to solve it.*

—Philip Friedman, *Grand Jury*

There is a way of thinking that works best when adults are at home around children. We call this family-way-of-thinking *FamilyMind*. There is also a way of thinking that works best when adults are engaged in a work/business/school setting. We call this work-way-of-thinking *WorkMind*. These are two dramatically different ways of being in a group.

To bring these two ways of thinking into clearer focus, make two lists beside each other, one with the heading "FAMILY/Personal," and the other entitled, "WORK/Business/School." How do we have to think when at work? How do we have to think at home? Under the FAMILY/Personal heading, list how our thinking differs from a WORK/Business/School setting. Do the same with the other column.

Key Differences Between
Home & Work

FAMILY/Personal	WORK/Business/School
1.	
2.	
3.	
4.	
5.	
6.	
7.	
8.	
9.	

From our readers, audiences, and the couples in Don's therapy practice, the following lists were compiled:

Key Differences Between
Home & Work

FAMILY/Personal	WORK/Business/School
1. tired from work	relief from home
2. personal needs	more objective
3. chaotic	more orderly
4. children & adults	adults

5. emotion/sex/intimacy

emotion/sex/intimacy
not appropriate

6. lots of activities in
different directions

activities toward a
single focus

7. housework/no pay

financial incentives

8. co-worker/needs

spouse/needs

9. personal care

production

When we compare these two lists, the different themes become clear. At work or school *with other adults*, we focus on goals to provide services, attain a degree, or produce a widget. Our purpose at work is to accomplish and to produce. At home we focus on the needs, wants, and wishes of ourselves and our *children* to provide the care we all need to survive and thrive as individuals and as a family. Our purpose at home is to love, be loved, and to belong. Producing care is different from producing widgets.

"When I'm at home, and I feel tired, I can probably find the time to put my feet up. At work I have to ignore my fatigue and get on with the project."

"Working around adults on the job allows me to have an entirely different mind-set than when I'm around my children at home. It's sort of like the difference between driving down the freeway and seeing two lanes of traffic at work and watching four lanes of traffic at home."

"I know my boss cares about my welfare, but his bottom line is profit. At home my personal needs *really* matter. Like that saying, 'If Mamma ain't happy, ain't nobody happy'!"

"I've always thought of my home as a place where we give care to each other. I give care at work, too, but it's on a more impersonal level, so we can get our job done."

"Because I'm not paid for doing housework, it's hard to have much respect for my job. A salary tends to give work a *real* quality, somehow."

"It's sometimes a relief to go to work, where I know my desk will be in the same order it was when I left yesterday."

"Intimacy at home glues us together. Intimacy at work can blow the whole place apart."

Where we are determines our thinking mode. The environment shifts our focus from a **service** orientation at work to a **care** orientation at home. The problems of learning to belong and work together in a family are made clearer by understanding the differences in thinking and attention required within the home and work environments. We must clearly know what the job needs from us at work, what the family group needs from us at home, and not mix apples and oranges.

Apples: Attention and the Workplace

The workplace is the modern-day equivalent of the premodern hunt. It is designed to produce products and services reflecting the goals of a particular business. Real estate companies link people wanting to buy or sell houses; the phone company provides communication services; a plastics manufacturer makes food containers; a hospital provides medical care and rehabilitation, and so on. In a similar fashion, premodern hunters were driven by a singularly focused goal—feeding their tribe. These hunters were carefully chosen according to their skills to fulfill necessary roles for survival. Similarly, modern employees are carefully selected to complete the tasks necessary to meet the goals of the company—products and/or services—to stay in business.

The mindset of the hunt or the workplace is *single-focused*. On the job, we work among adults who strive to be cooperative and competent to complete the agreed upon goals. Most of us are relatively free to focus on our tasks with few unrelated disruptions to lead us astray. We are expected to be able to leave our personal lives—illness, worries about children, relationship problems, and so on—at home, or at least outside the business door. Our bosses count on us to function productively in spite of our personal roles and responsibilities. Like the hunters of old, our focus and attention must be tuned to what is necessary for meeting the bottom line—what the business needs to be profitable, to survive and thrive. Effectiveness lies in the ability to narrow our focus, to give our full concentration to the task at hand.

> *I can hear sound in fine detail. It's just like what they say about people who live in the rain forest—"Gee, they're sitting there eating their dinner and all of a sudden they hear a sound that no one else can hear and they pick up their spears and they bring home tomorrow's dinner." It's the same thing. It's learning to listen to the relationship of something within something else....There's nothing supernatural about it in the rain forest the way those guys learned....They grew up listening like that.*
>
> *If I'm sitting in my house, I mind what colors the walls are a lot. I mind where there's light. I mind if there's a lot of clutter in my vision. I mind what it looks like a lot. If I'm sitting in the studio, I don't care. I can stay in there fifteen hours at a stretch with no windows. I don't care if there's a jumble of wires on the floor. I care if the couch I'm sitting on is comfortable and that's about it. And I care if I can hear.[1]*
>
> *—Linda Ronstadt, singer and recording artist*

Modern business is realizing that goods and services are not the only things that count. People matter, too. Employers know that workers with good benefits, pleasant working conditions, and room for showing creativity and independence are more loyal, cooperative, and productive. Satisfied employees are willing to give their best to meet the bottom line.

WorkMind

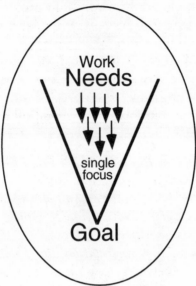

In the work/business/school setting *we line up our personal needs with the work goal. For that period of time we have a single focus.* The guiding question is, "How can we, as a work group, line up our needs and resources to meet this goal?" In a service-oriented work situation, the element of care must be present but is centered around the working needs of adults, independent adults who take care of their own personal needs so their attention can be focused on their work responsibilities. Care in the home is an entirely different way of thinking.

Oranges: Attention and Home

The premodern hearth or camp was the center of the community, holding family members together. We use it as a metaphor for the modern home. Families gathered nightly to discuss personal matters of care with each other. Here they considered the needs of the group, what the family needed to survive. From these gatherings the goals of the hunt were determined. The hearth was the touchstone of meaning, the holder of the heart life. From here the ancient hunters entered the outer world to sustain the inner needs of the people. The hearth gave the hunt meaning and purpose. *The hearth was the reason for the existence of the hunt.*

The major difference between the workplace and home is the presence of children. Let us say that again. *Children, completely dependent upon adults to provide care for their physical, emotional, psychological, and spiritual needs, make home totally different from work.* These needs are enormous, never-ending, and both predictable and unpredictable.

> *My best friend tried to explain how my life would change after Bryan was born, but I just didn't get it. My husband and I were living the "good life," you know, lots of dinners out, movies, parties, that sort of thing. We expected to fit the new baby into our activities and busy work schedules. How wrong could we be? Babies need your undivided attention.*
>
> —*Jessie, thirty-two, mother of two*

The mind-set of the home is multifocused and hearth (heart) centered. Children require a diffused attention. The minute we focus on a task requiring our undivided, or single-focused attention— Brrrrrring, Brrrring, Hooooot, Hoooooot—bells and whistles go off, alerting our offspring to the fact that they are no longer in the spotlight. How many times have our young children been playing quietly and we think, "This would be a good time for that phone call I have been trying to make for days."? Two minutes into the conversation, we are interrupted with an urgent need for a drink, something to eat, a band aid. Dusting or cooking allows a less-focused attention, but the minute we sink down on the couch with an interesting book, "Mommmmyyyy. I neeeed you. I just can't wait!!!!" Effectiveness at home lies in the ability to do several tasks at once while keeping the needs of the group continually in mind. In the family setting, *we line up goals to meet the personal needs of the family* *and its members. For that period of time we have a **need** focus.* The guiding question is, "What does this family **need** now, including me?"

FamilyMind

In the workplace, care, a single focus, and an understanding of the bottom line are all utilized to produce products and services. At home, multifocus, products and services, and *knowing what the group needs* are combined to generate care. Without knowing this fundamental difference between the workplace and home, we drive home from work, come through the front door, and begin mixing apples and oranges—hunt-mode thinking with hearth-mode needs.

A mother thinking in WorkMind after she gets home from her job will get things done but will probably miss her own needs and those of the individual family members in the process. She is guided by the WorkMind question, "What do we have to do to get things done?" The scenario goes something like this:

Mother thinks, "OK, first I'll put in a load of laundry, and then I'll start the grill." She yells at the kids, "Joanie, Sandy, hang up your coats and empty your lunch boxes! NOW!" While thinking and shouting, she is systematically collecting and putting away the clothes, cups, books, and mail that were left out this morning in the hurried dash to work and school. The kids, meanwhile, are in the family room, fighting over which TV program to watch. As Mom hurriedly stuffs clothes into the washer, Sandy wanders in with tears in his eyes and a red streak just under his cheekbone. "Mom, Joanie hit me with the remote," he wails. Mom groans, "Not now, Sandy. You two work it out, while I get dinner ready." Sandy stalks back to the family room, revenge on his mind. On the patio, lighting the grill, Mom hears a blood-curdling scream from Joanie. She rushes in to find her daughter hurling pillows, magazines, books, anything within reach, at her brother who is crouched under a table. "Enough!" roars Mom. "Both of you, to your rooms. Do your homework, and stay there until dinner time." She flinches at the angry looks from her children. With a deep, tired sigh, Mom finishes cooking dinner, knowing what eating the meal will be like with a tired, hostile family.

At home, when one of the parental leaders functions in a Work-Mind, single-goal-focused way of thinking, she or he gets out of sync with the whole purpose of home—the meeting of personal needs. If one mode of thinking gets out of hand, unrealistic expectations are created that leave everyone going in different directions and unmet needs overwhelming even our best efforts. In the previous scenario, Mom followed the four points to WorkMind thinking:

1. Motivated by goals and achievement

2. Task-focused

3. Impersonal actions

4. People expected to follow orders in an adultlike manner

When we shift from WorkMind thinking to FamilyMind thinking, we work together to get what we need and want. Let us play the scenario again, as Mom uses the FamilyMind question, "What does this family need now, including me?" as her guide.

Mother thinks, "OK, there's laundry to be done, and dinner to be made, and the kids have their chores and homework to do. What do we need first? I'm tired and hungry, and I'll bet the kids are, too." On her way to the kitchen, she collects cups and mail that were left out this morning in the hurried dash to work and school. She calls eight-year-old Sandy and ten-year-old Joanie to the kitchen as she sets out cut vegetables and dip made that morning. "Ugh! I hate veggies," grumbles Sandy. "There are soft pretzels in the freezer, if you want to help yourself," says Mom, as she sits down and stretches out her tired legs. She and Joanie munch on veggies, while they talk about their days. Sandy hovers silently in the background, making his pretzels. Sensing something is wrong, Mom asks, "Sandy, what do you need right now?" "It doesn't seem fair that I have to fix my own snack." "Oh, you wish there was something you really like to eat to sit right down to." "Yeah, how come I have to do all this work?" he complains. As the three continue to talk, Mom discovers that Sandy has had a particularly bad day, first losing his homework, then speaking out of turn in class, and then fighting with his best friend over a game during recess. He needed consoling and nurturing. Joanie needed Mom's help with a part she was learning for tomorrow's play auditions. Mom needed to do at least one load of laundry, so she'd have a particular blouse to wear tomorrow to an important meeting, and she wanted to get to bed at a decent hour to read a new novel she had just started. Dinner was yet to be made, tomorrow's lunches had to be packed, and homework had to be done. Because she knew that being outside was nurturing to her son, Mom asked Sandy to pick some lettuce from the garden for dinner. Then she asked Joanie to put a load of clothes in, while she started the grill. As she made the salad, Mom coached Joanie with her part, while Sandy worked on a homework project at the kitchen table. What was accomplished and whose needs were met? Homework was finished; Mom learned about her children's day; Mom's blouse was ready for tomorrow; dinner was made; Sandy felt heard and understood; Joanie was seen and supported; Mom enjoyed the time she spent with her children.

In this scenario, Mom used the four steps of FamilyMind thinking to ease her family through a difficult transition—the time between getting home from the day's activities and bedtime.

1. Motivated by love and care

2. Need-focused

3. Personal actions

4. People contribute according to their abilities

By asking, "What does this family need now, including me?" Mom used the tasks—laundry, getting dinner, homework—as places and moments to connect with her family. They accomplished what needed to be done to make a home run smoothly while giving care to one another.

Celebrate the Small Stuff

When we consider that family members connect most often around household tasks, those tasks become valuable moments; moments when our son might ask in an off-hand way, "Where do we go when we die, Dad?" Or our daughter might wonder, "Mom, did you ever smoke?" These valuable moments are what the Spanish call *milagros pequeños*, little miracles. They are opportunities for connection that do not come often and may never come again. These holy moments open the doorway to the soul of our family, where a common heritage unites us. They contain what we are all desperately seeking: belonging to a group in a meaningful, caring, and joyous way. Just across the threshold may be the key to our daughter's depression or our son's stubbornness. These little miracles come naturally when parents see household tasks as meaningful moments, as places to connect, and as times to really see each family member's needs, wants, and wishes.

◁▷ ◁▷ DON | I hate to mow the lawn, but I'm always the one who does it. My son is allergic to grass, and Jeanne has knee problems. Just recently I've become allergic to grass, too, and I feel terrible for several days after mowing. Consequently, I procrastinate until the yard needs to be scythed and baled. One day in frustration, Jeanne suggested I hire a neighbor boy to mow for us. At first I felt threatened. "I'm a man. I can mow that yard!" After I calmed down I asked, "What does this group of people really need now including me?" I realized my manhood was not being threatened at all, and that was the best five bucks I ever spent. Jeanne said, "Thanks for getting the job done." I took a nap.

FamilyMind: A Series of Little Miracles

When we ask, "What does this group of people need right now, including me?" we go right to the heart, the soul, of the family. FamilyMind thinking allows us to live in the present moment, conscious of our own needs and the needs of those around us. Because we are open to the emotions and feelings—the heart life—of our children *and* ourselves, we are open to the little miracles that happen between us.

I now have a name for my condition when I get home from my job: WorkMind Hangover. It takes a couple of hours for the last project to stop going around and around in my head. The problem is that my wife and kids get home several hours before I do, and my wife needs help with them and getting dinner. It's like having to be a tag-team wrestler; I have to jump right into the ring as soon as I get home. Rather than being helpful, I was distant and distracted, and my wife became angry and resentful. When we talked about what we both need after work, we found similar needs: to be outside, to do something physical, and to be free not to focus attention on anyone else for awhile. After our talk, we changed our evenings. My wife gets home, sets the table, and helps the kids with their homework. When I get home, she's out the door for a twenty-minute jog, while I go outside with the kids to wrestle, throw a ball, or take a walk to the duck pond. By the time we're back, my wife can take over while I soak in a hot bath and change clothes. Then we all help get dinner. We have to be very flexible, but working together to get all our needs met has made a wonderful difference in our evenings together as a family. My wife gets alone time and exercise; I get time with the kids, and alone time; the kids get attention; and we all work together on something we all need and enjoy—dinner!

—James, thirty-three

GroupMind: A Series of Unlimited Choices

WorkMind and FamilyMind are complements of each other and are two vital, normal ways of thinking when people are in groups. Without the first, we would accomplish nothing, and without the other, our needs would not be met. Wherever we are, we continually move in and out, back and forth, from the goal focus of work to the need focus of family and back again. As we discussed earlier, the setting we are in determines the degree to which we use a particular thinking mode. At work or school, we use WorkMind a greater percentage of our time. At home, FamilyMind is more often necessary. Both places demand flexibility and the appropriate thinking mode for the moment.

Understanding WorkMind/FamilyMind has helped me tremendously at my job. I love to talk, anywhere. But at work people constantly tell me I talk too much. I'm very good at what I do; I won't be fired for talking; so I've basically ignored the feedback. I figure they're just being uptight fuddy-duddies about their work. After thinking about it, I realized that the problem is not that I talk too much at work, but that I talk too much about personal things. When I go on and on about my family relationships and others' troubles, I distract myself and others from their work. I always knew something was off, but I just ignored it. Now, I see I need to cut back on the depth I go into about my dating life and other personal things, to save that for talk with my friends outside of work. I will always love to talk, but I hate to admit that limiting the personal talk makes us all feel less uncomfortable, and I get my work done faster.

—*Michelle, twenty-seven*

A *Raising a Family Seminar* participant tells the following story: "My wife and I both have offices at home, mine upstairs, hers downstairs. When I need to talk with her, I have to go down the stairs and through the kitchen/family room to her office. One day after working on a report for several hours, I marched down the stairs, through the kitchen, and past my young son, who was snacking at the dining table. I walked into my wife's office, put the report on her desk, walked back through the house past my son, up the stairs, into my office, and sat back down at my computer. I felt funny, until I realized that during the entire walk from my office and back again, I was hashing over a problem in my head. In WorkMind mode I had walked through FamilyMind space, and something hadn't felt right. I had completely ignored my son and had hardly acknowledged my wife. In an office setting, I could have walked by the desk of a co-worker without saying anything, and this would be considered normal behavior. At home the same behavior is rude. I went back downstairs and sat down with my son to say hello. Then I knocked on my wife's office door and apologized for being so distracted. Our connection felt warm and reassuring. I felt so much better when I returned to my own office."

WorkMind and FamilyMind can be mutual friends or mutual enemies. When we work outside our homes, we are most often engaged in WorkMind thinking unless we call home, take a break, or think about our families with FamilyMind thinking. The work environment dictates our mind-set, just as the needs of small children do at home.

Children use WorkMind thinking when they concentrate on a project whether they are at school or at home. Drawing a cartoon or building the tallest block tower takes a good deal of single-focused thinking. When we consider the school as our children's workplace, we see how they learn to weave back and forth between the two ways of thinking— WorkMind to accomplish something, FamilyMind to interact with others and to get needs met. At home, parents go in and out of these thinking modes, too, with hobbies, yard work, financial record-keeping, and so on. GroupMind thinking offers us unlimited choices for relating to others, with WorkMind thinking when we have to get things done and with FamilyMind thinking when we have needs to be met. Our thinking moves like the Tao, ever changing from one to the other, as the need arises, with the seeds of both implanted deep in each heart.

GroupMind

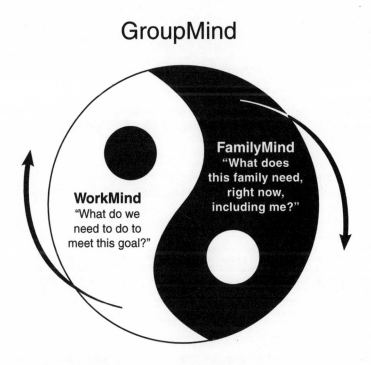

FamilyMind
"What does
this family need,
right now,
including me?"

WorkMind
"What do we
need to do to
meet this goal?"

Wherever we are, we must consciously attend to which mode of thinking is needed. We must know *what* we need, *when* we need it, *how* to switch modes of thinking when necessary, and *how* to discuss all this with our family members.

Endnotes: Part Two

1. Joel Selvin, "Ronstadt Proves She Can Go Home Again," Datebook, *San Francisco Sunday Examiner Chronicle*, 19 March 1995, 25.

PART THREE

Living in FamilyMind

"Well," said Owl, "the customary procedure
in such cases is as follows."
"What does Crustimoney Proseedcake mean?"
said Pooh.

—A.A. Milne, *Winnie-the-Pooh*

Sure, I come home every night, and my kids love me,
but somehow I don't really fit. You know? My wife and
I make all the big decisions together, and we agree on
most stuff, but it seems she still runs the house. We all
look to her for the little important things about home.
She complains that I'm somehow just not there, but I
don't know how to change that. I don't know what she
wants me to do.

—Jon, twenty-nine, father of two

Rather than *doing* something new at home, FamilyMind requires *thinking* something new. Not simply a tool to get us out of the middle of a big fight with our spouse, Family-Mind requires a shift of perception. It is like choosing a new way to eat for the rest of our lives, rather than going on diet after diet after diet. Imagine changing from one pair of eye glasses to another; one pair gives us strength to see the world in terms of products and services: plans, lists, goals. The other pair gives us the power to see in terms of personal care: needs, wants, and wishes. At work we put our personal needs aside to meet goals. At home we create goals to meet our personal needs.

Seeing in FamilyMind

Consider the dilemma of deciding where to go on the family vacation, that bastion of family togetherness. The kids say they'll die if they don't go to Disney World; Mom's idea of a real vacation is vegetating on a sunny beach; and Dad likes the challenge of a fancy dude ranch in Idaho. How do they choose a holiday the whole family will enjoy? With their goal-oriented glasses, this family may go through many ideas—Disney World this year, the beach next year, and Idaho the year after that. Or, maybe Mom and daughter should go to the beach, and Dad and son should go to the mountains. Would flipping a coin work? What if it came up "heads" for Disney World, and Mom just cannot stand the thought of lines, noise, and cotton candy? Must she make the supreme sacrifice of a few days in paradise to fulfill her children's wildest desires? Or do she and Dad grapple behind closed doors, making the ultimate decision that everyone has to live with, no matter what?

Let us look at this stalemate through the glasses of FamilyMind. We begin by editing the FamilyMind question, "What does this group of people need now, including me?" to fit the situation: "Concerning our vacation, what do we in this family group REALLY need, individually and together?" What is Dad's desire to go to a dude ranch really about? What needs would such a trip fill? Why does Mom want to relax on a tropical beach? What needs would be met for her? What does Disney World promise the kids that they feel they cannot live without? After a lively discussion, we find that Dad really needs to do something adventurous but not dangerous, something out in nature that is exciting and challenging. Mom really needs to rest, to let go of the stresses of daily work and family life, to be nurtured in a beautiful setting. The bottom line for the kids is that there be fun things to do, no chores, and no babysitters. Everyone wants to be together.

Looking at genuine needs enables this family to step outside of the limiting perimeters of dude ranch, beach, and fun park. More importantly, it helps them let go of the cultural "shoulds" about taking family vacations. Perhaps everyone's real needs would be better met by making changes in everyday life that provide what these family members thought they could get from a vacation. Dad might need to spend some weekends in nature—fishing, rock climbing, or horseback riding. Mom could use some nurturing during the week to learn to relax—a nap, yoga classes, a massage. The kids want to spend more family time together having fun—perhaps family night stargazing, after-dinner story time, or a family band. When it is time to make vacation plans, the family won't feel so pressured to have it all in one huge trip. Maybe now Mom can handle that trip to Orlando, or perhaps the family looks at other options, such as a camping trip on a lake, where needs for nature, relaxation, and fun can all be met. The point is that this family is guided by their *real* needs to have a vacation, rather than by the cultural ideas of what a vacation *should* be. Perhaps they will see to their everyday needs for rest, fun, and adventure, rather than saving it all up for a vacation. Looking through the glasses of FamilyMind shows us many choices and alternatives we may have never noticed before.

REALLY Needs

Asking the question, "What does this family need now, including me?" is the first part of FamilyMind. How do we answer the question? How do we know what we, ourselves, and others REALLY need? On the grand scale of life, we all need and want the same things—love, safety, care, intimacy. But, does safety mean the same thing to us as it does to the person sitting across the breakfast table? We all want to feel safe, but what makes one person feel safe may make another terrified.

> *Having an orderly house is satisfying and makes me feel safe. Having a neat house reminds my husband of how things were at home when he was a child, and he wants to run!*
>
> —*Jennifer, thirty*

My girlfriend loves to drive fast. She says she feels safer and more in control when she's keeping up with or exceeding the pace of other drivers. It makes me want to get out and walk.

—Jack, nineteen

Timothy always kept a gun in the drawer by the bed. He wanted to be prepared, he said, for anything that happened. He felt safer with a gun. I loathed the thing and trembled inside every time I thought about it being there.

—Nina, forty-three

Assuming that we know our family members' needs and mistakenly believing they are the same as our own is the major obstacle to making a family work. Acting from wrong assumptions leads to misunderstandings, hurt feelings, loneliness, and betrayals. When a wife says, "I need to rest," her need could be filled in a number of ways. Maybe she needs to lie down and actually go to sleep; or her need might be met by meditating under the wisteria arbor in the garden. Her husband finds tending to his plants restful. If the two of them are working together on some project and she says she needs to rest, and he finds her later outdoors sketching a rose bush, he might think, "Oh sure, she needs to rest, rather than working with me!" His hurt or angry feelings come from his different interpretation of "rest."

The following story from a friend of ours beautifully describes how differently family members can interpret the same event. "My sister and I just had our fortieth birthdays. But, it was a very weird thing. I found out that my mother wanted to throw a surprise party for us, and I was mortified. I am acutely embarrassed about being made a fuss of, if I haven't earned it. As an identical twin, my sister and I always got far more than our fair share of attention, without doing a thing—by just walking into a room. When a fuss is made over me just because I look exactly like someone else—who I adore more than any living creature on the planet—I feel embarrassed about it. Twinsomeness seems to encourage people to forget their manners, make ridiculous comparisons, and ask all kinds of intrusive questions. We hated our birthday parties when we were little. Having now turned forty, we really didn't want a party, but our mother said, "But, darling, it was the most important day of my life!" That's when I said, "Let's have the party FOR YOU!" My stunned mother said, "Okay." And that's what we did. The big party was her need to acknowledge the biggest day in HER life, not ours. I can't tell you the relief I feel now that we did that for her, and it was a great party! My mom is very special! My sister and I are elated—we are finally free of this yearly, dreaded affair."

This is FamilyMind thinking at its best: finding ourselves stuck in a family interaction or expectation that is always miserable and using the FamilyMind Question to look more deeply into what family members REALLY need. The results from making decisions and choices from "really need" may look a bit unusual, but the activity or event then has meaning. The family in the previous story discovered that its members did not feel the same about a time-honored event—the twins' birthday party. The mother was showing her love and joy by giving a party, assuming that her daughters felt the same way as she did; the twins experienced this caring as annual family torture! Now they can celebrate *together*, each one getting what she REALLY needs.

Knowing What We REALLY Need

> So, based on your theories, when my kid is with me in the checkout line, yelling, "Give me some candy. I REEEEALLY neeeeed it!" I buy it for him, right?
>
> —Vern, forty-two

We must have food, water, shelter, and touch to survive.[1] Modern families with children are consumed with the tasks of providing enough of these vital needs for each member to live. When faced with a hundred choices of candy flavors, textures, and shapes, or with two dozen laundry detergents making two dozen promises for a cleaner wash and an easier life, it is no wonder we lose touch with what we REALLY need.

So often I find myself doing things just because someone else wants to do them. My husband gets really frustrated when he asks me what movie I'd like to see or what I want to order for dinner. I usually say, "Oh, you decide. It's so hard for me to know!" When I ask myself what I want or need, I come up blank, like there's nothing there.

—Gloria, fifty

Why is it so hard for us to know our needs, wants, and wishes, our feelings and preferences? The answers lie in two directions: first, our life experiences—the abuses and traumas we all suffer—teach us to lose touch with our inner selves and we forget how to check in to see how we feel; and secondly, our consumer-focused society trains us from birth to look outside ourselves for the keys to happiness.

Even with our parents' best efforts, the traumas of our birth, our infantile sensations of cold, hunger, loneliness, and pain, and our first attempts to fit into a world of adult rules and cultural expectations leave many of us focused outside of ourselves. From birth we learn that our needs are not as real or as urgent as we think they are. Parents are cautioned to delay answering our cries, so we won't be spoiled; we are weaned at two months, because Mom is pressured to go back to work; we are potty-trained at three, because the preschool requires it; when we fall down and scrape our knees, Dad says we're not hurt, so we learn to ignore the pain and get back on our tricycles to please him; we sit for hours in front of the TV, silently absorbing the violence, racism, and consumerism, because it is the cultural pastime. These early lessons leave us either unable to focus inward on our own needs or unable to focus outward to hear the needs of others. Most of us go in and out of a mixture of both, leaving us clueless about our own and others' genuine needs, wants, and wishes.

When we do not recognize our deepest needs, we look to others to tell us. The American media has insidiously accepted the responsibility of informing us what will bring happiness and satisfaction to our lives. A sleek, new car confers social status; the right perfume assures sophistication; the latest fashion label offers sexy allure; the newest gadget insures more leisure time, and so on. We are convinced to buy what we think we should want, but many of us feel empty, overworked, directionless, and alone, surrounded by a whole lot of stuff. We are unable to give anything to others because we are so needy ourselves. We are stuck in the never-ending cycle of wanting more, *More*, **MORE**! And yet we yearn to be seen, heard, and valued for who we really are, rather than for what we own, how we look, what work we do, or who we know.

Our use of technology has steadily eroded what healthfully holds a family group together: the soul life—what has purpose and meaning for the group, what we REALLY need. What common ties unite us; what ideas, causes, and values rally us as a group; what ingredients determine our love and loyalties? The hearth or heart life, where family members work together for mutual care, belonging, fun, and meaning, has become a meaningless battle with time, ruled by the clock, the calendar, the egg-timer, the coach's stopwatch, the TV schedule, and online computer services. Therapist and author Mary Pipher, Ph.D., graphically describes our situation in her best-selling book, *The Shelter of Each Other*: "Time is a boundary that's been blurred. Shops used to be closed on Sundays and after six at night. Town whistles signaled when to rise, eat, and go home for lunch and dinner. News and weather were broadcast in the morning, at six, and again at ten. Everyone's life had more or less the same structure. Now television channels broadcast nonstop and every small town has an all-night convenience store. Banks have twenty-four-hours-a-day, seven-days-a-week automatic teller machines."[2]

Somewhere during our technological discoveries, we allowed our machines and consumer products to dictate our desires, and we became deadened to the soul's deepest preferences, needs, wants, and wishes. How do we reconnect with these doorways to the soul—our source of aliveness—and bring hope, meaning, and joy to our families?

The Soul's Identity: The Feeling Life

The soul is reflected in our feeling life. By listening to and under-standing our feelings, we become more in touch with the soul's purpose. With conscious effort we can become more soulful, that is *filled with soul*, and we become more able to know and understand ourselves, to use our inner wisdom, and to create our lives through purposeful choices. We become more sensitive to others, more empathetic, and better able to help them get what they need. The Greek writer Nikos Kazantzakis wrote that there are three kinds of souls with three kinds of prayers:

1. I am a bow in your hands, Lord, draw me lest I rot.

2. Do not overdraw me, Lord, I shall break.

3. Overdraw me, Lord, and who cares if I break.[3]

The longing that many of us experience is the longing to know ourselves as parts of God, to do good works, to live good lives. Our souls lead the way. The soul lies just outside our intellectual understanding. We cannot know our souls by collecting data or through scientific reasoning. We learn to know and live from our souls when we allow ourselves to risk standing alone on our principles, to be challenged to do something unknown, to do the right thing even when it is difficult. To continually allow ourselves to be the instruments of good will, creative thought, and positive action increases our ability to touch our souls and the souls of others, and to grow. The messages from the soul come to us in many ways:

1. Likes and Dislikes: In our waking life, who we really are is communicated through our preferences, our likes and dislikes, passions, and hatreds. "I like clothes that fit just right." "I prefer the beach over the mountains." "I hate well-done steaks." "I like indirect lighting." "I don't like to be yelled at." "I feel scared when our bank balance gets below one hundred dollars." "I like to be outside as much as I can." "I feel out of control when the house is a mess." "I am afraid to disagree with my friends' ideas." Telling someone that our favorite color is blue appears to be an innocent and insignificant piece of information. However, the way that information is interpreted and used can mean the difference between feeling connected with another person or feeling shut out and alone.

My favorite color is blue. I have a closet full of all shades of blue. I never wear purple, because my skin turns yellow in purple. What does my husband give me for our anniversary? A purple negligee! I felt so alone. After fifteen years of marriage, he still doesn't know me.

—Tara, thirty-seven

I thought my wife liked every color. She looks good in anything, so I didn't give it much thought. When she opened the box, I knew I had blown it. She tried to seem pleased, but you can always tell. She was hurt. At first I thought to myself, "Oh, here we go again. She's just so picky!" Then I realized that I had missed something very important. I had failed to see what she really likes, to understand who she truly is. I felt so isolated, like I lived on another planet.

—Ben, thirty-six

2. Opening Our Hearts to Another: Most of us have had the experience of mulling a problem over and over until we become totally lost in our thoughts or feelings. How wonderful it is to share the issue with friends or family members and have them say just the right thing. Their words may not solve our problem, but hearing, "I understand you," or "You really feel strongly about this," or "How can I help?" touches a place deep within each of us that is truly nourishing, restorative, and enlivening. We feel seen, heard, supported, and understood. By talking with someone who really tries to hear us, we often clarify the muddle we were in. The person listening to us has touched our soul, and the soul tells us what we REALLY think and feel.

3. Being in Silence: To know ourselves or another, we must watch and listen very carefully. We do not have to study ancient texts or make pilgrimages to obscure holy places to hear the soul. We must simply become quiet, watch, ask, and listen to our own inner messages. Being silent does not come easily for most of us used to the hectic pace and noisy backgrounds of our technological lives. We are continually bombarded with beeps, bells, horns, sirens, radios, TV, and the sounds of construction, destruction, and repair. We are subject to the demands of deadlines, project reports, relationship expectations, family schedules, and household upkeep. Is it any wonder that our busy minds have difficulty letting go? With patience and persistence, the regular practice of meditation, prayer, taking walks alone, even fishing, opens a channel to the deepest parts of ourselves, where our "REALLY needs" lie hidden.

4. Dream Messages: At night, in the language and images of our dreams, the soul communicates to us like bubbles rising from the bottom of a deep, still lake. These needs, wants, and wishes from the unconscious part of ourselves come coded in pictures, symbols, and colors that, with interpretation, have meaning to us. Traditional cultures the world over regard dreams as precious gifts, to be shared each morning upon awakening. They can be harbingers of some future event, warnings that our present endeavors and attitudes are leading us astray, or glimpses of who we truly are.

We must each discover our own special ways to find the truth within us. Someone we know found his answers through learning contemporary and ancient poetry; a bookseller friend relates to the truth she reads in novels and history; we know an artist who finds solace in the meditative state of painting; a grandmother uncovered many truths during a weekly quilting bee; gardening is a balm for a neighbor; and Angeles Arrien, Ph.D., anthropologist, author, and teacher, encourages finding our truth through the time-honored practices of standing meditation, walking meditation, reclining meditation, and sitting meditation.[4] Without the vital information of what we REALLY need, we experience soul loss; we lose touch with ourselves and with others.

Author Sandra Ingerman writes in her helpful book, *Soul Retrieval*, that "...almost everyone I have ever met suffers from some sense of incompleteness and emptiness. They sense that parts of themselves are missing and that they are cut off from a deeper connection with life.

For some people, this feeling of incompleteness and alienation causes great suffering. For most, the sense of not being fully alive is a continual, low-grade pain often masked with drugs, entertainment, compulsive sex, and addictions of many other kinds.[5]

I knew something was wrong, but I didn't know what it was, and I didn't take time to really follow my feelings. I guess in some funny way I really didn't want to know. The clues were there, so obvious that I could have stumbled over them—that I needed to listen to and focus on our relationship. In a very odd way, I was relieved when I found out my husband was having an affair. That place in me that knew came to the surface, and I felt better and worse at the same time.

—Mari, forty-one

From birth, my son was difficult. He cried for the first six months of his life, and he has been a trial ever since. The first thing I noticed about him was his tenacity— the first time I looked in his eyes, he was right there, regarding me as if to say, "Well, what challenge do you have for me today?" All through his childhood, he stubbornly hung on to his own ideas and ways of doing things. He opposed his father and me from the get-go. I wish I had realized then, that this quality was a gift of his soul, something innate that would see him through the rough times in his life. Back then we were always at odds. Now I know that he needed our support, our encouragement to do things his way. He finally gave up on us, and I haven't spoken to him for five years. I hear he is doing well as the director of a home for troubled boys. He doesn't give up on them.

—Tracy, forty-nine

I live in an urban area where my children were born, where I have a thriving business, and where my family has many friends. But when I think of the hills of North Carolina, something cries out inside of me, some part that longs for green, quiet, a slower lifestyle, and Home.

—Audrey, thirty-nine

The problem is not that we don't have a sense of what is deep within our souls. The problem is that we have trouble verbalizing it, reflecting upon it, and taking action. These are skills we can learn.

Endnotes: Part Three

1. Ashley Montagu, *Touching* (NY: Harper and Row, 1978).

2. Mary Pipher, *In the Shelter of Each Other* (New York: Grosset Putnam, 1996), 85.

3. Nikos Kazantzakis, *Report to Greco* (New York: Simon and Schuster, 1965), 16.

4. Angeles Arrien, *The Four-Fold Way* (San Francisco: Harper San Francisco, 1993).

5. Sandra Ingerman, *Soul Retrival: Mending the Fragmented Self* (San Francisco: Harper San Francisco, 1991), 18-19.

PART FOUR

Give'ntake—Loving with a Whole Heart

Love is effortful.

—M. Scott Peck, M.D., *The Road Less Traveled*

Remember the butterflies-in-the-stomach feeling, that rush of excitement when we saw him or her, the we-can-do-anything-together fantasies we had when we were *in love?* We felt full of life, ready to tackle any obstacle, protective, gallant, forgiving, and *romantic.* Where did it all go? Romantic love offers us glimpses of the "promised land," of being connected to something greater than ourselves, but it cannot take us there. Romantic moments lift us out of our everyday world into a land where all dreams seem possible. They are special, inspiring, and invigorating, yet these ecstatic experiences alone do not provide the spiritual sustenance we need to meet the difficult situations in daily family life. Relationships in a marriage and family cannot endure only with the magical feelings of romantic love. All too often we judge the states of our marriages and families by comparing our feelings with a Cinderella-and-the-Prince kind of loving. All too often we are disappointed. The fiery passions that once consumed us have cooled. The person we wake up beside in the morning sometimes seems like a stranger. We wonder where our Prince or Princess has gone. Rather than a life lived happily ever after, we are left with someone we are sometimes not so sure we want to be around, dirty underwear, furniture with water rings, piles of credit card bills, a sixty-hour work week, little league practice, and oil stains on the driveway. Or we are just left, period; left alone to deal with the kids, the house, a job, and trying to get on with our own lives. The love that we thought would be transformed into a strong, sustaining bond, that would help us face the inevitable conflicts of relationship, has eluded us, leaving us lonely and in despair.

If Romantic Love Doesn't Work, What Does?

Romantic love brings a couple together. It helps us see the perfection in each other. It offers us wonderful fantasies of what life can be like. Let a bit of reality creep in, however, and little doubts begin to cloud our sunny world. The stress of overwork and fatigue, an annoying habit, or an illness may make us wonder what we ever saw in this person. Perhaps, for many reasons, we don't get the support or care we need and expected from our object of romantic love. Perhaps our mate also needs understanding and nurturing, and we have no more to give. Not knowing that love requires us to work together to develop a lasting love, we want to bail out, jump ship, fly the coop, hoping to find that perfect love we long for with someone else.

The love a family needs to sustain itself through life must be based in practicality. It must be accessible at any time—in the middle of an argument at one o'clock in the morning; when our child breaks a favorite dish; when our teen pierces his nose; when our ex consistently brings the kids home late. We need a love that takes us through and beyond our anger, shock, disappointment, and grief to connect us with something much more powerful than the fireworks of romantic love, a love described by a friend of ours as *give'ntake*.

> *Giving and receiving is really one word, give'ntake. A family won't work when you make it two words. Sometimes you lose track of which part of the word you are acting on, but when something is seriously off, you can be sure that the solution lies in getting the two words back to one.*
>
> *—Wally, father of three*

Give'ntake love is an act of loving, rather than being romantically *in love*. By responding to the FamilyMind Question, "What does this family need now, including me?" with chosen actions based on need, the energy begins to cycle between the people involved. That cycling energy is what we sometimes call love—connected to each other from deep down inside. This love is not an accident. It is available for those who choose to act. It is a whole love involving two parts— giving *and* receiving. Giving others what they genuinely need, want, and wish for awakens the love in their hearts; receiving what we need from others permits our love to flow. Give'ntake love allows an intimacy that makes a person feel genuinely seen, heard, and given to by another. It is a shared experience that many spiritual traditions call *oneness*—a feeling of being so close to another that we no longer feel separate.

If love were excluded from life, all souls in the world would

assume externality to each other, and their only possible

relations and contacts would be superficial and mechanical.

It is because of love that the contacts and relations between

individual souls become significant; and it is love which gives

meaning to every happening in the world of duality.[2]

—Meher Baba, *God to Man and Man to God*

BEWARE: This elusive feeling of oneness is not to be confused with feeling *so one* with another person that we expect him or her to be able to read our minds. As therapists and transpersonal educators, we often hear: "She should know how I feel about that; we've been married for fifteen years!" "Why didn't he know I needed to rest instead of working in the garden?" "She knows I love her. I shouldn't have to say it all the time." "He still doesn't really know what style of clothes I like. Do I have to sketch it out for him?" These statements and questions indicate a wish to be known and understood the way we thought we were as infants.

Then, it seemed to us that our needs were met without our having to ask. Because a baby cannot tell us what she needs, we as parents have to work from moment to moment to figure it out. When she cries we check to see if she needs changing, feeding, burping, walking, rocking, cuddling, entertaining. When we finally discover her need and meet it, the baby feels warm, safe, content—loved without her having to ask for it.

How much easier it would be if our babies could tell us what they need, want, and wish for. Fortunately, most of us become very good at figuring out just what our babies need. Usually our skills serve us well until our child is seven or so, after the will struggles into being. Then we usually find that "talking about it" provides us clues that make our guesswork much more accurate. With our help, as our children grow, they get better and better at telling us what they need, want, and wish for. As our understanding of them grows, our level of intimacy with them deepens.

On some level, we all long to be understood and cared for like we were as infants. Intimacy cannot develop, however, on the efforts of mind reading or guesswork.

> *Now I understand why my husband was so frustrated. I constantly complained that he never gave me what I really wanted from him. I gave him the message that if I had to tell him what I wanted, it really didn't count. So he was always guessing, and he's really not a very good guesser where women are concerned. I'd get fruitcake when I wanted flowers, a back rub when I wanted to make love, a new oven when I wanted crystal. No wonder he felt so alone and isolated from me.*
>
> *—Kate, fifty*

The pathway to true intimacy—that oneness or connection we all long for—is through communication, caring, persistent questioning, and action about what we really, really need. Listening to other family members, asking questions to be sure we understand their needs, voicing our own needs, and acting on the information we discover lays the foundation for intimacy in relationships—give'ntake—loving with a whole heart.

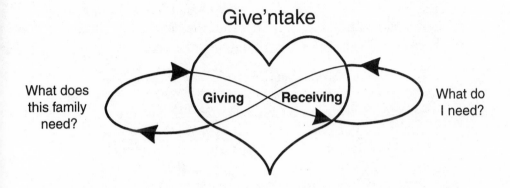

Give'ntake love offers solutions to the problematic interactions of any family configuration—single parent, intact biological, foster, gay/lesbian, step, and adoptive. If it is so simple, why don't we all do it, all of the time? Before we are able to freely give and receive, we must recognize how we get stuck on one side of give'ntake or the other—the states of mind we call *overgiving* and *overreceiving*.

Getting Stuck on One Side: The Habit of Overgiving

Overgiving is giving more than is required or needed. It is giving to others to the exclusion of ourselves. Overgiving is a habit that is developed to solve a problem. For example, some of us as children, tried to be very, very good to escape the notice of an alcoholic or abusive parent. We learned to overgive to protect ourselves from harm. Those of us who were born first in our families may have feared we would get lost in the hierarchy of family membership and learned to overgive to insure our place of importance. Children of divorced parents or parents in turmoil may learn to overgive in an attempt to bring peace to their families. As adults, we continue to overgive to others to survive within relationships. When we continually protect our three-year-old from falling off her tricycle, repeat-edly cover our teenager's absence at school, persist in financially bailing out our young-adult daughter, we overgive out of love for our children. Because we give more than is truly needed, we cripple our children with a false sense of entitlement; they lose the opportunity to take risks; and they fail to learn from their mistakes.

> *My sister was given everything she wanted, or thought she wanted. She chose an expensive women's college, so my folks sacrificed their vacations for her. She dropped out after a year and a half, and came home to live. My folks sent her to Europe for six months, thinking she might grow up a little. She got in with a bad crowd there, and started using drugs. She came home really a mess, so my folks paid for a long-term treatment program. After she got out, my sister moved from job to job, boyfriend to boyfriend, never quite making it, with my parents financially filling in the gaps. It was only after she had her first kid that my aunt helped her see that she had to be responsible and accountable to someone; if not to herself or my folks, then to her baby. Somehow my sis straightened herself out. She went back to school, got a Ph.D., even. My folks helped out with the child care, of course, but since then she has been able to handle things pretty much by using her own resources. She still has to ward off too much help from my folks.*
>
> *—Jeff, brother of Jennie, twenty-seven*

What happens to us when we habitually overgive? When we over-give, and slow down enough to look inside ourselves, we feel lonely, underappreciated, overworked, resentful, tired, and trapped.

> *I worked a fifty-hour week for years with little time off for vacations. Usually my family took trips without me, because I chose to work. I thought I was doing it for*

them, so the kids could have those fancy skateboards, clothes, and a good college fund. When I decided to retire early, I was shocked at my family's response. First, they seemed glad to have me more available, but soon they became afraid they couldn't buy everything they wanted; then they got angry when I wanted something new, or wanted to choose a vacation site. They seemed to resent my being at home, too. I ask myself what all that hard work and sacrifice was about.

—Len, age forty-five, father of three

The Christian teaching, "It is more blessed to give than to receive," has been misinterpreted by many of us. We learn that giving is good; receiving is bad. We become depleted, because we are unable to allow others to give to us, and we deny our need to receive. When our children are young, it is very easy to get trapped in the extreme end of giving. The endless feedings, diaperings, washings, and other tasks leave us running on empty and longing for a respite, time alone, and a week of continuous sleeping. We can get too tired and too stuck to even know what we need, let alone ask for it. How blessed we are when reminded by a loving spouse, sibling, in-law, or friend to take care of ourselves. Giving is the heart of love, but it is only one half of love. *To truly give what others need, we must be able to receive.*

-43-

Getting Stuck on the Other Side:
The Habit of Overreceiving

Those of us who grew up poor or deprived never received enough food, physical care, or emotional love. Consequently, we may be so empty we feel our needs can never be filled. When we become so focused on our own lives that we fail to be mirrors for our children, they may grow up without the limits and structure necessary to learn an awareness of and an appreciation for another person's reality. As adults, these children are too focused on their own needs for constant attention, reassurance, and support. We, as parents stuck in overreceiving, often give our children the message, "You're not good enough." Having Dad consistently turn the attention away from his daughter to focus on what *he* thinks she should do, or on what *he* thinks is right instills the belief, "I'm not good enough for Dad to listen to what *I* want. I'm not good enough to take up space, to be heard, to do things *my way*." Over time a sadness sets in, and a child chooses one or several coping behaviors: she may give up; she may become an overreceiver herself; she may become an overgiver trying to win Dad's affection and attention; she may get depressed; she might act out for any attention she can get by skipping school, doing drugs, staying out after curfew, throwing tantrums, refusing to eat, and any of the other various and amazing ways we humans find to fight against or adapt to our life situations.

Being stuck in the habit of overreceiving is as difficult as being stuck in the habit of overgiving. We think we want attention, but what we truly long for is to feel connected, especially to our mates and our children; to be understood, to be cared for, to have our genuine needs met. We want to be able to say, "I hate this," and have someone respond, "Tell me more so I will understand." For many of us, however, the pain of connection is so great that we shield ourselves from the very contact we crave. We do not share what we think, feel, or believe, because in the past our opinions were met with coldness, anger, denial, sarcasm, ridicule, disbelief, or contradiction. The trust necessary to be open to another person was crushed within us. Children, who never experience having an adult stoop down and try to see the world through their eyes, develop a great rage and rebelliousness and become stuck in seeing things only from their own points of view.

> *I should have recognized the early signs, but I was too much in love at the time. During our engagement, I asked Caleb one evening to help me with dinner. His reply was, "What! Is this a test, or something?" I guess I should have been testing him, because now that we are married, he does nothing for anyone in the family on his own initiative. When we ask him for help, he gives only grudgingly. He acts like a child who never got what he needed, and he refuses to admit that anyone else might need help, or love, or compassion. He seems to have totally given up on human connection and has no idea of what it takes to make a relationship work. And no matter how much he takes, he's still miserable.*
>
> *—Judith, forty-two*

Being stuck in the habit of overreceiving leaves us like the beautiful Narcissus, isolated and caught in the love of his own reflection.[2]

We continually misunderstand others and are misunderstood by them, because we cannot see anything beyond our own needs, wants, and wishes. We feel empty, because only half of our hearts are working.

Before Don told me about this FamilyMind thing, I came home from work, put my feet up on the couch, and read the paper until dinner time. Sometimes, I even took a nap, saying I needed this time to unwind from my busy day. I had a constant battle with the kids to leave me alone and to be quiet. At dinner my wife was uncommunicative, even hostile, glaring at me over the roast beef. Dinner was always loud, demanding, and ended in indigestion for all of us. Some days I just didn't want to go home.

—Ron, thirty-two, father of three

A person who takes and gives without considering what others need is difficult to be around for very long. This is why small children are so exhausting and why we must teach them generosity, empathy, and a willingness to see things from another person's point of view. They learn these admirable traits best by following our lead, modeling our behavior, rather than heeding our lectures.

Overhearing my daughter's play with friends, I was dismayed at her bossiness and overbearing manner. She talked constantly, never letting anyone else add their own ideas or make suggestions about their play. Later that evening with all the family home, my husband said quietly to me, "Jena, you're doing all the talking! I've been trying to tell you something important for several hours." Then our son popped in, "Yeah, Mom, you're always ordering us all around. Set the table! Pour the drinks! Do this! Do that! We can't get a word in anywhere."

—Jena, forty-three, mother of two

A three-year-old, wailing loudly because she wants to carry the pet rabbit's cage to the backyard, when the cage is as large and as heavy as she is, cannot make room for explanations or other suggestions. The world through her eyes is the cage and her struggle to wrest it away from her big brother. She cannot see that the cage is too heavy for her to carry alone, or that her brother is trying to help. Her narrow focus only allows her to know she is not getting *her way*. Fortunately, when allowed to be the center of attention and to see life in their own way, three-year-olds pass through this necessary stage of being stuck in the needs of self. Some of us grow to adulthood, however, never having learned that others have their unique needs, often different from our own. We become stuck in an overreceiving state of mind, keeping us detached from the family and out of the rhythms of giving and receiving. We may find that family members side against us, and feel cheated and overpowered by our presence. Children whose parents are stuck in the overreceiving part of give'ntake, may feel small and unimportant at home but bloom at school, where they get the attention they need.

> *Jeffrey was polite and alert, but very quiet in class. I worried at first that he had a hearing or seeing problem, because he just couldn't seem to keep up in a discussion, answer a question, or complete an assignment from the board. One day I asked him to tell us about his favorite thing to do after school. He beamed and talked nonstop for about ten minutes about his hamsters and iguana. From then on, he became an active member of our class. After meeting his family and reviewing his past records, I realized that he was given very little time or space at home to voice his own ideas or opinions. Both parents came home tired from long jobs, and there were four children to be cared for. Jeffrey blossomed under the class's interest in his life outside of school.*
>
> —*Juanita, thirty-two, fourth grade teacher*

Getting Stuck:
You Can't Get There From Here

When a parent is caught in either extreme of giving or receiving, conflict, competition, and revolt erupt from all members of the family group. When we recognize our habitual ways of getting stuck,

FamilyMind becomes easier. All of us tend to begin on one end or the other of the give'ntake scale. Do we usually approach problems and situations from the point of view of what others need or want? Or do we seldom consider another's perceptions and experiences and act from our own agendas? How we respond to others is a habit that inadvertently leads us into power struggles, arguments, and win/lose situations. It helps to know our stuck spots—where we err on either end of the scale—to bring ourselves back into what is happening in the moment. By knowing our patterns in difficult situations, we increase our options of response, freeing us to consider the needs of the group and ourselves. The truth of this discovery became clear for Don on a family vacation in Mexico.

  Don | We were speeding down a paved but very narrow road with no shoulders in a rented VW bug. I was the self-appointed leader in this family outing in search of a secluded beach where friends had told us there were hundreds of conch shells for the taking. I felt like a tank commander in enemy territory with a precious cargo. The traffic ranged from slow, gawking tourists to hell-bent taxi drivers, and the bug's shock absorbers responded like silly putty. I fought to find a safe speed between the 80K (55mph) speed limit and the 100K (80mph) of the local drivers. Too slow and we would be run over; too fast and we may blow the engine or bounce off the road. After a few miles along this treacherous route, without their saying a word, I knew my family was beginning to freak out. As the tension inside the little car grew, I imagined their criticism. "Now they're going to tell me I'm driving too fast, it's not safe, and give me advice about how to drive better. I'm the one who cares enough to drive and get us there safely. Why can't they just let it go and support me?" On and on my mind went down the path of they-don't-value-respect-care-love-understand-and-appreciate-me, and no one had said a word!

Then my step-daughter, in a trying-to-be-caring-and-not-critical-but-I'm-scared-to-death voice, said, "Don, this car sounds funny. It's bouncing around and feels very unstable. Are you sure you should go this fast?" Before I could say anything, Jeanne said, "Honey, we don't have to be in such a hurry."

I felt the anger rise within me as I clenched my teeth to bite back the I'm-the-driver-and-I-will-get-us-there-safely-if-you-would-only-butt-out lecture. In the past, this was the moment when I would either yell, "Let me drive!" or slowly move to the shoulder of the road and calmly say something like, "OK, then *you* drive!" This time the road didn't have a shoulder, and cars were zipping by like bullets. Suddenly, my mind shifted. Rather than asking my usual question, "Why are these people so screwed up and unappreciative of me?" I asked myself my new question, "What does this family really, really need right now, including me?" I had shifted into FamilyMind thinking. My anger melted, and I asked my step-daughter, "Tell me when I am going a speed that feels safer to you." I let my foot gently off the gas pedal until she responded, "There, that's fine." Then I asked Jeanne what speed felt right to her. She wanted me to go a little faster to avoid troubling the drivers behind me, so I sped up and checked the new speed out with my step-daughter. Both she and Jeanne were satisfied. My son, trying to tease his sister, said, "I want to go real fast, Dad!" My step-daughter's boy-friend added, "Yeah, let's see how fast this thing will go!" Their impish grins made us all laugh, easing the tension, and the VW bug now seemed to be gliding rather than bouncing along. I asked, "Is everyone OK now?" The answer was a unanimous "Yes!" Then I delivered the news. "Guess what? We are now traveling the exact speed we were a few minutes ago when everyone was upset." After the laughter and "No ways!" died down, I realized how using the FamilyMind Question had altered my usual response to include the feelings of others in the car. I could listen to the real needs beneath their words, "I'm scared. Please consider me, too." My real goal for the day was to safely find the conch shell beach and have fun with my family. Locked in my own little world, however, I couldn't get there from here!

On reflection, I realized speed was not the real problem in the vacation adventure. Speed was what my family group focused on to explain their out-of-control feelings. They felt out of control, because of me, the self-appointed leader—because of my focus. On the outside I was "Dad, the Tourist," having a carefree time. But not on the inside. On the inside, I was in my single-focused, WorkMind hunter mode: Destination—Conch Shell Beach. ETA: 14:00 hours. Attent Hut! Move Out! I wasn't even aware of it. I was in my own little world, playing out my old habit of leading like a platoon sergeant. Under battle conditions and clear objectives with trained soldiers, this mode of operation saves lives. Under family conditions with spouse and children, it always ends in "Kill the Leader." "Why?" I asked myself. The answer was clear—a family's needs are not military objectives. Families run on care, and out of that care come the goals. We reached Conch Shell Beach at 14:00 hours. We didn't find any shells, but I brought back a special souvenir—that a difficult family situation can be resolved when family leaders and members use care and real needs as the most important signposts to guide them to their chosen destinations.

"Kill the Leader:" A Signal to Re-Group

Being able to love with a whole heart creates emotional access to each other and especially to us, the adults in charge. The accessibility of the leader allows family members to think, "I can feel safe. I am included. Dad will consider my wishes, wants, and needs, and together we'll work it out the best we can." When, as leaders, we isolate ourselves by staying in our own little world—like Don was without knowing it—group members begin to feel cut off and out of control. They begin to feel unsafe. It is only a matter of time until someone in the group revolts and confronts the leader.

Challenging the leader can be a good thing. No one has fun, especially the leader, if group members are feeling afraid and left out. Bad feelings always come out one way or the other. Often, the first confrontation is indirect—jokes, sarcasm, whining, rowdiness. Someone may get hurt, having learned that injury moves parents into a caring mode. If these overtures do not nudge the leaders awake into FamilyMind thinking, an open revolt occurs with blame, judgments, and name-calling from family members. When the leader responds with harsh or domineering tactics, group reactions are predictable, following any number of unpleasant routes: Family members pull back, become quiet, and stew until later; they create subgroups with other members, talk about the leader problem, and plot against him or her; some literally walk away from the group and go their own way; or others make an appointment with a marriage counselor or a divorce attorney. If we have a long-standing reputation as an inaccessible leader, family members will plot how to get out of the group. Spouses may dream of divorce, a different mate, or of being single forever. Children may dream of the day they turn eighteen or of running away from home.

A game of "Kill the Leader" signals a drop in the group's feelings of trust and safety. Members ask themselves, "Will Mom (or Dad) consider my wants and needs, even if they sound silly?" The quickest way for the parental leaders to stop the game and reverse negative feelings is to shift into FamilyMind thinking. To do that, we must return to the question, "What does this family need now, including me?" Again, this basic question helps us shift out of a domineering, competitive, isolated mode of relating into the place between giving and receiving, the rhythmic give'ntake that fosters genuine care for other family members and ourselves. The "Kill the Leader" game changes from threat to an opportunity. The leader now has the opportunity to refocus, to regroup by including those who felt left out and afraid.

Extreme giving and extreme receiving are as common as rain and sun. The nature of life includes the extremes. Getting stuck in either extreme is what leads to big problems, but FamilyMind brings back the opportunity to open the heart. The "Kill the Leader" response becomes the door through which lies the experience of being held in that special emotional and spiritual embrace of meaningful belonging.

Psychological Labels

The popular names for overgiving and overreceiving in psychological terminology are co-dependency and narcissism. The problem with psychological labels is that they diminish who we are into something small, cramped, concrete, factual, and limited. Labels shut the lid on the unlimited, ineffable, numinous qualities of the human spirit. Narcissism and co-dependency can describe our behavior in a given moment in time. These names, however, do not capture all of who we are and all that we are capable of. Seeing our behaviors as habits we developed at some point in our lives to solve a problem we were then facing, gives us room to change. If in one moment we are stuck on one side of give'ntake, in overgiving, for example, we can open to the possibility of moving from our stuck place toward a more balanced position of giving and receiving. If we think of ourselves as co-dependent, and that's just how we are, there is very little room available to us for change. We are stuck in loving with only half a heart.

Learning a New Habit:
Loving with a Whole Heart

hab-it, n.: a. A recurrent, often unconscious pattern of
behavior that is acquired through frequent repetition.
b. An established disposition of the mind or character.

—American Heritage Dictionary

Loving with a whole heart means having access to both sides of give'ntake—giving *and* receiving. Give'ntake loving is also a habit learned through repetition in response to situations in our lives. Like the learning of any new habit, it takes time, focus, lots of practice, and much compassion for self and others.

When work gets backed up, I forget about giving and receiving. All I can see is the next form to be filled out, the next phone call to be returned, the next client to be seen. My family life sort of fades into the background. I come home drained, no energy left to think about what others need. I leave my snack dishes in the bedroom, forget to feed the cat, leave the lights on all over the house, expect to have dinner ready for me, leave my clothes lying around, and my mind is so full, I don't hear when my kids talk to me. My wife said that she tried to get my attention one night after dinner, and I walked out to the garden as though I hadn't heard her. I hate being so out-of-it and isolated from everyone. After I realized I'd been so spaced, I consciously did something with each of my kids, and my youngest said, "Dad, where have you been?" Life's too short for that!

—Vince, thirty-nine

The foundation of give'ntake love is the FamilyMind Question, "What does this family need right now, including me?" It can be repeated like a prayer or a meditation mantra—being spoken softly in the background of our minds, reflected upon when we are alone, and discussed with other family members. This new habit of loving with a whole heart is strengthened and deepened through focus and repetitive practice to eventually become an "established disposition of the mind or character."

All of us are born with the capacity to give and to receive. Within a family, however, we have to learn how to give and receive in direct proportion to the needs of ourselves and others. It is a habit we must consciously learn. Loving with a balanced give'ntake requires loving in the moment. We must let go of our old expectations of love—a perfect romantic love, being loved like we were as infants, making things equal, having no conflict, being constantly happy, and so on. Give'ntake love is a conscious act from one person's soul to another person's soul. Give'ntake love can not only heal the past but enlivens our current family relationships with a rich connectedness and aliveness. Through give'ntake loving we learn to live in direct contact with our family's soul. We have direct access to who we are and who we may become.

Give'ntake

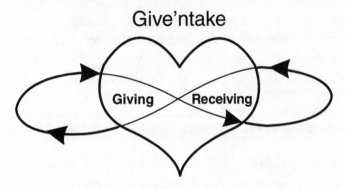

For one human being to love another: that is perhaps the most
difficult of all our tasks—the ultimate, last test and proof,
the work for which all other work is but preparation.[3]

—Rainer Maria Rilke, *Letters to a Young Poet*

FamilyMind Question, "What does this family need now, including me?"

Solution: Loving and being loved with a whole heart.

No matter how hard we try, sometimes we stay stuck in our old, ineffective ways of dealing with conflicts—our old habits. Even when we ask the FamilyMind question, we may continue to be stuck on one side or the other of give'ntake. We must discover what gets in the way of being able to love with a whole heart.

Endnotes: Part Four

1. Meher Baba, *God To Man, and Man To God*, C.B. Purdom, ed. (North Myrtle Beach, SC: Sheriar Press, 1975), 265.

2. Thomas Bulfinch, *The Age of Fable* (New York: New American Library, 1962), 135.

3. Rainer Maria Rilke, *Letters to a Young Poet* (New York: W.W. Norton and Co., 1962), 53-54.

PART FIVE

There's A Hole in My Sidewalk

...We are taught you must blame your father,
your sisters, your brothers, the school, the teachers—
you can blame anyone, but never blame yourself.
It's never your fault.
But it's ALWAYS your fault, because if you wanted
to change, you're the one who has got to change.
It's as simple as that, isn't it?

—Katharine Hepburn

We each bring our old habits of giving and receiving into every relationship we have. Sometimes these old habits serve us well, such as knowing how to keep our anger from exploding all over someone else; using good listening skills; and responding without blame or judgment. Other old habits keep us from truly taking an active part in a relationship, such as blaming others for every bad thing that happens to us; running for the door at the first sign of conflict; or doing all the talking. Our friend, Laura Kennedy, M.A., therapist and anthroposophist, suggests that the work of our times is learning to balance the needs of the individual with the needs of the group. Many of our personal, psychological ways of relating get in the way of our being able to reach out to others or to love with a whole heart, and very often we have no idea what we are doing. We just wonder how we got here. Portia

Nelson's poem, *Autobiography in Five Short Chapters,* offers a simple and profound model of change that helps us identify our old habits that get in the way of give'ntake. When we understand these personal obstacles, we are free to relate to others from what we really, really need.

> **Chapter One**
> *I walk down the street.*
> *There is a deep hole in the sidewalk.*
> *I fall in.*
> *I am lost…I am helpless.*
> *It isn't my fault.*
> *It takes forever to find a way out.*[1]

How did I get into this family mess? Why does she treat me this way? Why am I always the one to pick up the house? Why do I have to tell him what I really need? What makes me so unlucky? Who keeps tripping me up? When did my life get so bad? These reactions come from genuine frustration of feeling that someone or something beyond our control is ruling our lives. These familiar questions support the belief that what goes wrong in our lives is not our fault. "Someone or something out there is responsible. It couldn't have been me. I'm trying as hard as I can," we scream to anyone who will listen. So many of us find ourselves in family situations we vowed we would never create; parenting like our parents did, being the same kind of spouse that our father was, staying in a job we hate like our mother did, and so on. We are genuinely stumped!

⊰⊱ ⊰⊱ DON | During a group discussion with twenty marriage counselors, I asked, "How many couples have you seen who say, 'I don't understand how things got this bad. I'm stuck with the same problems I had in my family as a kid. Our first year of marriage was so good, and now it's so bad.'?" Everyone laughed nervously, because we had heard this complaint, in one form or another, from every couple we saw, and as the conversation deepened, we each admitted that it applied to our own relationships as well.

As we walk down the "street" of family life, many of us find ourselves stuck in a deep hole with no idea how we got there and no clue how to get out. Because we did not consciously choose to be in this hole, it cannot be our fault. Many of us work very hard to ignore the hole we are in, blaming others for our predicament, and feeling lost, helpless, used, and frustrated.

"My boss piles so much work on me, I'm always behind!"

"My three kids make me constantly late."

"If only I hadn't gotten married, I'd have my own business rather than being stuck in this job I hate."

"The stress of my life keeps me hooked on drugs, alcohol, miserable relationships, overeating...."

"My mother smothered me, and my father was never home."

"Mikey did it!"

Chapter Two
I walk down the same street.
There is a deep hole in the sidewalk.
I pretend I don't see it.
I fall in again.
I can't believe I am in this same place.
But, it isn't my fault.
It still takes a long time to get out.[2]

Again and again, we respond before we realize what we are doing. Continually finding ourselves in the same hole and protesting it is not our fault indicates we are on "automatic pilot."

The world of sports clearly illustrates this automatic response. Tennis instructors are very careful to teach beginning students to grip the racket correctly. They know from experience that bad habits picked up early take hours of reminders and practice to unlearn. Coaches stress fundamentals in daily practice, because our first lessons, repeated over and over again while we are young, become automatic. During competition or under stress, we return instantaneously to our earliest learnings. The basketball player sees her chance and goes for the lay-up, making the weave, duck, and jump without thought. The lineman instinctively makes an opening for his quarterback. The center fielder automatically dives for a short pop fly. Intensive, repetitive training patterns become integrated into the human brain. When the appropriate stimuli appear, the brain reacts with the prescribed response automatically. Because the pattern is already present and thoroughly ingrained, little time is needed to consciously think about the situation.

Automatic responses are essential for athletes, soldiers, police officers, and others whose "split second" reactions may mean the difference between winning and losing, life and death. In our daily family relationships, however, the automatic responses we learned as children may lead us back into the same deep holes, where we struggle to understand how we got there and why. When we respond without thinking, our brains are activated to play the patterns we practiced as children over and over again. People and situations trigger emotional and behavioral memories, and we react to a specific *past* time and place and to a specific set of individuals. We find ourselves saying and doing things we do not want to say or do. It all happens so fast that it feels normal. It is not normal, but it feels so familiar we usually see no other options before us. Our responses may be totally inappropriate for the situation and may seem extremely out of place to others. One couple shared the following incident with us: Gerald spoke weekly to his aging parents, and his wife, Jeanette, sometimes joined in. After one call, Jeanette shared with Gerald, "Your father treats you like an idiot. How can you act so pleasant and appear to be so happy to talk with him?" Defending his father, Gerald told Jeanette she had her own "father issues" to work out. But later, Gerald was amazed when, during the next phone call, he really listened closely to how his father spoke to him. "He does treat me like an idiot!" he told Jeanette. "Now that I look back on my childhood with him, he always did. I guess I simply adjusted to it. It felt normal." Although we may not want to respond the way we do, the patterns are all too familiar. After all, they helped us to adapt and survive. These habitual responses are formed to relate to a particular group of people—family—in a specific place—home—during a specific time—childhood.

> *My father was a mixture of different people. When he was drinking, he was a tyrant, ranting and raving about everything and everyone. When he was sober, he was kind and jovial, the father anyone would have loved to have. When he drank, I tried to be very small, staying out of his way or doing everything I could to please him. I grew up being very quiet, helpful, and agreeable. There are times in my life with my husband, who is a lot like my dad, when I need to speak my mind, say what I think, stand up for myself. When he is angry, though, I shrink inside of myself and hide. I assume he will act just like my dad did when he was angry. I don't want to respond this way, but there I am before I know it.*
>
> —*Marianne, thirty-seven*

Our automatic responses, such as how we reacted to a parent when we were young, are not necessarily wrong or bad. They probably served us very well as protection against emotional and/or physical pain in childhood. In adulthood, however, these automatic responses limit our options, because we are "there before we know it." We fall into the dangerous tendency of making assumptions about the behaviors of others, and we act on them whether they make sense or not. We are lost before we know it. Give'ntake cannot happen. We are kept from being in the present moment; distracted from what we really, really, need; and unable to find out what other family members need, want, and wish for. Give'ntake becomes a reaction to the past. It feels empty, rather than a conscious giving, receiving, and loving.

In the previous story, Marianne was aware of her automatic assumptions, or "the hole in her sidewalk," after the fact. Many of us are not aware or accepting of our behavioral patterns at all. We ask, "Why does this stupid hole keep following me around?" We see our repetitive, unconscious behaviors everywhere outside of ourselves, and we blame others for what happens in our lives.

> *For years I had a recurring dream that haunted me until I finally understood its meaning. I am being chased endlessly by a figure enveloped in a huge dark cloak who is intent upon killing me. I run and dodge and try all kinds of hiding tricks, but I can never elude him or see his face. I awake drenched in sweat from this dream until I finally turn at the right moment and see his face. It is my own face, and I realize I have been running from my own weakness.*
>
> *—Richard, thirty-three*

Chapter Three
I walk down the same street.
There is a deep hole in the sidewalk.
I see it is there.
I still fall in...it's a habit...but,
my eyes are open.
I know where I am.
*It is **my** fault.*
I get out immediately.[3]

Most of us were taught to be discreet about what we liked and did not like. We learned that if we had nothing nice to say about something or someone, we should say nothing at all. It was not polite to say, "I hate that." We are sometimes astounded when our children so easily voice their passions and hatreds. "Should we allow them to be so verbal?" we wonder. Many of us grew up being afraid of punishment if we expressed preferences that were different from our parents. If they voted Democrat, we voted Democrat. If they liked to drive Fords, we liked to drive Fords. We learned to be afraid of expressing ourselves, because if we disagreed with someone, they may have thought we did not love them. We confused *loving as a connection* with *loving as a preference*.

Likes and Dislikes:
Hate is Not the Opposite of Love

When we love another person, we feel connected and intimate. She or he is accessible to us when we need comfort or help. The opposite feeling from *loving as a connection* is not hate but fear, feeling unconnected, or estranged. We might say, "I have lost touch with you. I don't know what's going on, and I miss you." When we express *love as a preference*, we are in touch with our partiality for something.

```
┌─────────────────────────────────────┐
│        Love as a connection         │
│  ┌───────────────────────────────┐  │
│  │   Love  ↔    Fear             │  │
│  │   Connection   Estranged      │  │
│  └───────────────────────────────┘  │
└─────────────────────────────────────┘

┌─────────────────────────────────────┐
│        Love as a preference         │
│  ┌───────────────────────────────┐  │
│  │   Love  ↔    Hate             │  │
│  │   Like       Dislike          │  │
│  └───────────────────────────────┘  │
└─────────────────────────────────────┘
```

"I love orange sunsets," we gush. Or, "This road stinks. I hate the potholes!" we complain. We make known our likes and dislikes, and our preferences do not necessarily affect our love for another person.

These two ways of loving work together to allow the full expression of who we truly are. When we honor our likes and dislikes within an intimate relationship we are most alive.

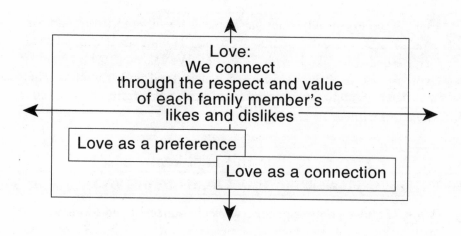

We are living in the present moment, and we can climb out of the hole in the sidewalk—our old habits from the past. Allowing another person to see who we really are—what we like and dislike—frees us to develop closeness and connection. Without it, we feel fearful, isolated, and alone.

After twenty-two years of marriage, my husband announced that he was leaving me and our two children and moving out of state. He refused to talk about the reasons, just deciding this move on his own. In therapy I had to face how I had gotten myself into this situation. I discovered that in those twenty-two years, I never really told my husband the truth about how I felt about him— about what I like and dislike. We both come from families who believed that roles were the guide for behavior, and that it was self-indulgent to worry about who you were as a person. If you were a wife and mother, that's what you did, according to the current definition of the times. My husband and I never took the time to get to know who we ourselves, or each other, really were by sharing our likes and dislikes. We looked like a successful family on the outside. On the inside, though, we both felt empty, fearful, alone, and had a longing to have the other know what we care about, like, and dislike.

—Dodie, forty-three

Knowing and respecting what we like and dislike helps us know what we want. When we know what we want, we can be proactive in our lives, rather than reactive, creating what we really need and want, rather than reacting to whatever happens to befall us. We end up in the hole in the sidewalk when we ignore our preferences. Our passions and hatreds, likes and dislikes, sympathies and antipathies are direct expressions of who we really are; they are communications from our soul. Through our likes and dislikes we are connected to our personhood and more able to follow our destinies. We stop living in the past. Rather than acting out our old habits from childhood, we learn to live in the present moment.

My husband goes crazy every holiday season. He ends up inviting his parents to visit for two entire weeks, because they live so far away. After five days we are all a wreck. I've tried to talk with him about what he really wants concerning his folks' visit, but I never get a straight answer. He feels guilty about the stress it puts on us, but his decisions are usually based on pleasing his parents, rather than on what we need. He falls so easily back into his childhood habit of trying to please his alcoholic parents to keep the peace. Although his folks have been "dry" for ten years, he still has a "knee-jerk reaction" to making sure they're happy. This year I asked him, "What do you like and dislike about your parents' visit?" After thinking for awhile, he said, "I like seeing them for the holidays, but I hate how stressed out we all get after five days." With that out in the open, my husband was able to consider options to simply suffering through his parents' visit every year. He discovered that they thought they would be more comfortable staying in a hotel for at least part of their visit, which relieved a lot of the pressure, and he even asked them to cut their visit shorter this year. Although his folks made a few negative remarks, they offered surprisingly little struggle to his suggestion that a six-day visit would suit us all better.

—Leslie, thirty-five

Some of our preferences change with time, some change moment to moment, and some live forever inside of us. Cathy, a young friend of ours, had a passion that almost ruined her, until she gave it room to be alive in her life. She says, "I grew up in the Midwest where I was taught that you do what's practical first, and then, if there's time, you can do what you like. One develops a lot of 'have to's' and almost no 'like to's' with a rule like that. We all did what we did, because it had always been done that way. When I went to college, I was expected to be a teacher, because my grandmother had been a teacher, and my dad had always wanted to be one. I, however, wanted to be a social worker. I pictured myself in the ghettos, helping people make their lives better. When my classes got tough, I went to my dad for encouragement. Instead, he counseled me against social work, because it was a struggle, jobs were hard to come by, and it might distract me from being a wife and a mother. He advised that teaching would always afford me a job if, for some reason, my husband was unable to work. Of course, there was no husband on the scene, but he was preparing me for the future that I was supposed to have. I became a teacher, taught for one year, and retired. My marriage fell apart—yes, I married the boy-next-door—and I was sick for two years. It took me nine years to realize that I got sick because I tried to make myself be someone I wasn't, to pursue a career I hated. During that time, I went back to school for an MSW degree, remarried, had two children, and now I work for the state child protective services. I'm out in tough neighborhoods helping people make their lives better, and I love it. It's not always easy, but doing what I love makes it all worth it."

Without meaning to, we parents sometimes expect our children to be just like we are. We cut off our children's link with their personal likes and dislikes, because we are unwilling to embrace their strong preferences, for and against. We take their hatreds as personal attacks, rather than as passionate expressions of who they are and what they need. Ironically, as the following story illustrates, when we make room for the "I hate you's," and try to hear what they mean, we restore connection, strengthen a sense of self, and sustain love.

We are very outgoing people, and from our daughter's early years, we were concerned that she seemed so shy. In a Raising a Family Seminar we were coached to go home and ask our daughter what she doesn't like about meeting new people. Her reply surprised us. "They are so big, and they put their faces right up to mine, and their breath stinks!" We responded as the Eliums had suggested by saying, "Tell us more." Our shy, little one went on and on about how she hated to meet strangers at parties, because they smile at her, tug at her, and expect her to talk, and she doesn't know what to say. We were amazed at how clear she was and how reasonable her dislikes were. Consequently, we became much more selective about our party-going, have fewer people at a time over to our house, and keep people from getting in her face. Tina is much more relaxed around others now, because I think she knows we understand and will stand up for what she likes and protect her, as much as we can, from what she dislikes. Compared to us, she is still shy, but she is making more friends at school and seems more at ease there.

—Edna, forty-six, mother of Tina, ten

Loving—feeling close, intimate, and connected to one another—requires the strength to voice and listen to the likes and dislikes of family members. In the heat of conflict, we all resort to the "I hate this" and "I love that" language. If we can train ourselves to hear these declarations as statements of preference—what we like and dislike about the person's behavior or the situation—we can avoid falling into our hole in the sidewalk, or at least, get out more quickly. We fall in when we ignore the likes and dislikes—our own and others. We get out when we take them seriously, listening to them with honor and respect.

Exercise

Take a moment to consider your family life now. What is it about your family that you like and dislike? Make two lists showing what you love and what you hate. Perhaps you hate the arguing that goes on just before dinner is ready. Or is bedtime with your kids an unhappy affair? Perhaps you love getting up in the mornings in a bedroom that opens out onto the garden, or the way you all sing together, gathered around the fireplace.

Preferences (loves/likes and hates/dislikes) around the house

*I love (like):

1.

2.

3.

4.

5.

*I hate (dislike):

1.

2.

3.

4.

5.

Now, complete the following exercise:

Preferences (likes and dislikes):
Discovering Your Soul and Your Family's Soul

Make a list of your many preferences—likes and dislikes—with the following categories as a guide:

- **Preferences (likes and dislikes) that you have had since childhood:**
    e.g. I have always loved (strongly liked) small animals and to this day I keep several pets.
    e.g. I still hate getting up early in the morning.

    1.

    2.

    3.

    4.

- **Preferences (likes and dislikes) that have changed since childhood:**
    e.g. I used to love (like strongly) the color red, but now I prefer blue when I have a choice.
    e.g. I used to hate classical music and now it's all I listen to.

    1.

    2.

    3.

    4.

On another piece of paper, complete the above list for your partner or significant other, and one for each of your children. Conversations based on the content of the evergrowing, everchanging family lists will allow love to grow.

Feeling Messengers

Having access to our feeling life is crucial, because our feelings help us really know what is going on. Being in touch with what we like and dislike tells us what we need and how we feel about what is happening around us. Our feelings act like a barometer, going up and down the scale of emotion, indicating how aligned we are with what we like and don't like. Emotions, such as anger, rage, hatred, joy, bliss, and excitement are feeling messengers from our souls that give us information about the situations we find ourselves in. So many of us learned not to show our feelings, or not to even *have* feelings. Feelings became the enemy, rearing their ugly heads just when we wanted to stay cool and rational. We have trained ourselves to be numb in situations that may trigger those dangerous feelings. What we did not learn to realize, however, is that feelings are simply signals alerting us that something is going on around us. We fear our feelings, because we might have to act on them, but that's the *last* thing we do in the feeling process. First we must recognize that feelings are wonderful clues to follow when we fall into the hole in the sidewalk.

Anger is a feeling messenger from the soul that tells us something is wrong. For example:

"I don't like it when you talk like that to me!" (Something is wrong in our communication.)

"This house is a mess!" (Something is out of order here.)

Sadness signals a loss of something we greatly value. For example:

"I missed the concert." (A fun opportunity was missed.)

"When will she come back?" (I am lonely for someone. I miss her company.)

Resentment indicates that we are being put in a position we detest. For example:

"I had to do last night's *and* this morning's dishes!" (I feel taken advantage of.)

"Why do you always ask my brother to help you, and you never ask me?" (I feel left out, unloved, unimportant to you.)

Joy says, "This is meaningful!" For example:

"I love cooking!" (I feel creative, useful, competent.)

"It was a wonderful day!" (Something inside of me was touched, nurtured, seen.)

Fear alerts us that something is trying to attack our core. For example:

"Please, don't leave me!" (I feel small, alone, and I need your help.)

"No, you can't make me do that!" (Something doesn't feel right; I'm not talented enough; I'm afraid to be seen.)

Anxiety moans, "I'm afraid I'm not big enough or good enough to handle what is coming." For example:

"What if I make a big mess?" (I feel horrible when I make mistakes.)

"No one else's parents make them come home so early!" (I must fit in; I'm afraid to be different.)

"Ohhhh, I get it!" exclaimed a workshop participant, after feeling messengers were explained. "When my wife shouts at me that I don't do anything around the house, she is feeling, maybe, resentful that she has to do everything alone. She could be really sad, too, because she wants us to work together, united as a couple. So I need to say something like, 'You wish I'd work with you.' Maybe then, we can avoid the hole in the sidewalk—the argument we always fall into. Ohhhhhh! So when we state a feeling, it is a message to look at what's going on in the moment, and it doesn't help to get upset about the feelings. They're really like friends who want to help. Ohhhhh!"

Feeling Messenger Dictionary

The following are aids in discerning the feeling messenger's guidance. The definitions are not to be taken as the only meaning, but a start in discovering what your particular feeling is telling you at a particular time and place about what is going on in and around you, your spouse, and your children.

Anger
Something is wrong. This is important to me.

Sadness
I have lost something greatly valued.

Resentment
I am being put in a position I detest.

Joy
I am involved in something meaningful.

Pleasure
This feels good (not necessarily meaningful).

Fear
Something is trying to attack our core.

Anxiety
There is more energy inside me than I am releasing.

Rage
I feel extremely scared, vulnerable, and hurt.

Add your own definitions and other feeling messengers that you discover.

When we have fallen in that hole and feel confused and stuck, we can use our feelings and preferences to tell us what is happening. We may think, "I feel angry right now, and I hate it when my wife criticizes me!" Or, "I feel proud. I like the way that project report turned out." Or, "I resent that he gets to go, and I have to stay home. I hate being the youngest!"

Feeling Boxes

Lions never thrive in captivity. Their native habitat demands of them an alive ferocity, an alert attitude, and a tender protectiveness. When captured and taken to zoos that do not sufficiently replicate their natural environment, lions often become aloof, depressed, and lethargic. Their natural "lionness" is neither welcome nor manageable in the zoo setting that does not reflect the wild, and they die a slow, tragic death. They look like lions, but they do not have the "feel" of lions. Their natural instincts are diminished by their adaptation to being boxed in or caged.

This same limiting process happens to many of us within our families. We learn very early in our lives what behaviors and feelings are allowed. In many families there is little room for a natural spiritedness, so our style becomes cramped, more docile. Other families do not allow anger or rebelliousness, and we are forced to put on a pleasant and agreeable countenance, no matter our inner feelings. Some of us grew up in homes where anger was the norm, and gentleness and tenderness were lacking. Some of us were not allowed to feel fear, hurt, or unhappiness, and automatic responses developed to accommodate these familial limitations.

No matter how well-intentioned our parents were, human life is so complex that some parts of each of us were bound to be left out or ignored. Like lions in captivity, we become boxed in and certain aspects of our natural selves are closed out.

‣ ‣ *Don* | Where and when I grew up, folks didn't know about psychology. Seeing a therapist was unheard of, and it was vitally important to keep any mental difficulties hidden. You didn't admit to drinking problems or depressions. No one I knew was educated about what fills self-help book shelves today. When I got to college and discovered the discipline and practice of psychology, I felt alive and relieved. Here was something that spoke to my heart, stimulated my mind, and fed my soul. Finally, I found a language and a way of thinking that explained what I had experienced and observed all my life that no one I knew in my community could articulate. This became my passion. At last I had a name for it!

To be able to recognize the holes in our sidewalk, to see with eyes wide open, and to get out immediately, we first must identify those parts of ourselves we left behind in childhood, those feelings that were not allowed in our families of origin or could not be named or valued in that place and time.

> *My father didn't think much of girls. As far as he was concerned, my sisters and I were there to work. If we had an opinion about anything, we were to keep it to ourselves, or suffer his humiliating comments about our stupidity, irrational thinking, and absurd notions. I learned to go along with what others thought and wanted, to squelch my own desires to fit the needs of others. Now, my husband feels constantly frustrated, because I won't say what I think or tell him what I want. There just wasn't room for that when I was a girl, and it's hard to change that old protective habit and let go of the fear of being ridiculed.*
>
> —*Margerie, twenty-eight*

Let us imagine we all have cages or boxes inside us where the feelings and behaviors allowed in our families are stored. We call these **feeling boxes.** On the outside of these boxes are the behaviors and feelings our families could not tolerate. Using Margerie as an example, her feeling box looks like this:

Feeling Box

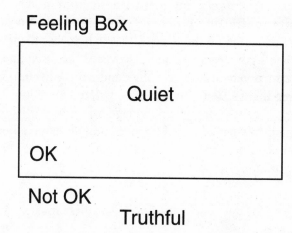

After understanding how intimidated she was from knowing her own thoughts, wants, and needs as a child, and with the support of her husband, Margerie learned to express her opinions and ideas. Now she can ask for what she wants and she can receive from others. Today her feeling box looks like this:

Feeling Box

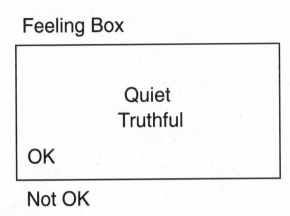

Quiet
Truthful

OK

Not OK

Belonging to a family is vitally important to most of us. When interactions are not based on each member's genuine preferences, those individuals must sacrifice parts of themselves to fit in. Each of us has left parts of our true selves on the outside of our feeling boxes and developed automatic behaviors to avoid having the taboo feelings. Some of us warded off anger through tears. Some of us were not allowed to feel fear and learned bravado as a front. Others of us were not permitted to have our own beliefs about the world and became either submissive or defiant.

My father died when I was young, leaving my mother with me and my four sisters. I became the man of the house and lost my childhood. I pretty much learned to take care of myself, because if I ever needed something, my mother acted worried and overwhelmed. After that I never asked for much and no longer thought I needed anyone's help with anything. I walled up any feelings of grief, need, or softness. I became very tough, resourceful, and resilient. That worked fine for me in the army, but now I have a wife and kids, and I don't know how to open up to them and to ask my wife for her help and support when I need it. I keep trying to do it all on my own, and I feel lonely, isolated, and left out of my family life.

—*Dale, thirty-six*

Dale's feeling box looks like this:

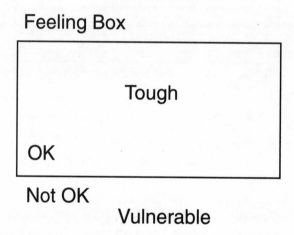

Exercise

To discover the contents of your own feeling boxes and the behaviors you developed to belong in your family according to the unwritten ground rules, take time to consider what feelings were not allowed in your family of origin. How did you have to behave to avoid trouble? What feelings did you have to deny or ignore to "act" appropriately? Fill in the boxes and discuss them with a close friend, a therapist, or your mate, if you want to. Are there suggestions or insights that may be helpful in pinpointing specific forbidden behaviors or feelings that fall outside of your feeling box? Remember to talk about these tender discoveries with caring and sensitivity. It is more helpful to offer insights as wonders or hunches, rather than as fact. "I wonder if anger was forbidden in your family, because you get so upset when I'm angry," is more easily considered than, "Anger was definitely taboo in your family. You can't stand my anger!"

Feeling Box   Name _____

OK

Not OK

Feeling Box   Name _____

OK

Not OK

After you and your mate have filled in your boxes, closely examine them together. Many couples discover that behaviors and feelings on the inside of one person's box are on the outside of the other's. Marriages and long-term relationships often involve a journey to recover our lost parts, and we may attract partners with feelings and behaviors we have lost within ourselves.

Now, think about how your children's feeling boxes might look. One family member's feeling box may look entirely different from another's. Perhaps it is more okay for Brother to show his anger but not his fear, whereas Sister is allowed to show her hurt but not her anger. Sisters and brothers often remember the same events differently, because they experienced them from different emotional positions. Gender, temperament, birth order, family circumstances at the birth, and so on all contribute to what feelings and emotions we are allowed to have in our families.

Feeling Box   Name _____

```
┌─────────────────────────────┐
│                             │
│                             │
│                             │
│ OK                          │
└─────────────────────────────┘
Not OK
```

Feeling Box   Name _____

```
┌─────────────────────────────┐
│                             │
│                             │
│                             │
│ OK                          │
└─────────────────────────────┘
Not OK
```

Feeling Box   Name _____

```
┌─────────────────────────────┐
│                             │
│                             │
│                             │
│ OK                          │
└─────────────────────────────┘
Not OK
```

Feeling Box   Name _____

```
┌─────────────────────────────┐
│                             │
│                             │
│                             │
│ OK                          │
└─────────────────────────────┘
Not OK
```

Naming

I have met the enemy, and he is us.[4]

—Pogo

According to many ancient, esoteric teachings, a person's name describes their essential qualities.[5] By conferring a name we give recognition and power. If the name or label is a negative one, those qualities are called forth. For example, when, in our public school system, children are described as "difficult" or "slow," they often live up to these labels that follow them throughout their school careers. Calling our childhood habits, "the hole in my sidewalk," allows us to take a few steps backwards to see its characteristics from a more detached viewpoint. When we give our habits names, we bring them into the light, reclaim them as parts of ourselves, and gain understanding about them. With knowledge comes power. We may have extremely difficult parts inside us to discover—forgotten secrets, anger, grief, or depression—but finding them and owning them gives us new power to relate with them. We get in touch with what we really, really need. If "they" are "them," I make myself a victim and end up at the bottom of the hole in the sidewalk. If "they" are "mine," I have more influence on my life. I am no longer at the mercy of mysterious outside forces. If I know how I truly feel, I am more able to give and receive within my family and am more willing to feel love and belonging. Using the information from your feeling boxes, name the hole in your sidewalk in five words or less. Here are some examples to help you:

"Cries when angry."

"Cleans house when scared."

"Blames others when hurt."

"Yells when feeling helpless."

Honoring likes and dislikes, listening to the feeling messengers, and recovering lost parts help us get out of the hole, because ignoring them is how we fell in.

Another Aid: FamilyMind Thinking

If you do fall into that hole in the sidewalk, there are several things to remember to help you find your way back out:

1. **Listen**—listen to the feeling messenger in the moment.

2. **Look**—look at what you like and dislike about what is happening.

3. **Feel**—allow yourself to feel those feelings that were banished in childhood.

4. **Love**—don't forget to love with the *whole* heart, or give'ntake.

In Part Four we saw how many of us learned the habits of *over*giving and *over*receiving to survive the trials of growing up. When we give with half a heart or receive with half a heart, we fall in that hole. Knowing where we fall on the continuum of giving and receiving frees us to come to a more balanced place, using FamilyMind. With the graph that follows, decide which state of mind you often "find" yourself in.

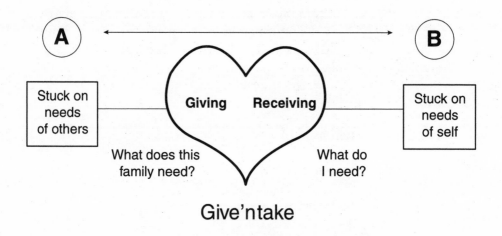

Are you closer to B, or do you tend to react from somewhere near A? Knowing you are inclined to get stuck in your own needs, or B-like, helps you know your own trouble spots—deep holes in your sidewalk—and shift back by asking the FamilyMind Question, "What does this family need now, including me?" If you tend to consider the feelings of others to the exclusion your own—an A position—then you need to shift toward A—thinking of yourself, too. Here is an example:

Both of your children begged to have pets, promising they will take care of them. Remembering how much you loved your childhood dog, you give in, and now your family has a turtle, two bunnies, and a puppy. They are all adorable, and your sons follow through on their promises pretty well—for awhile. After several days, you find you now have full responsibility of the turtle and the puppy. What do you do?

Do you choose:

1. to continue feeding the pets, knowing the chores are difficult and take away from your sons' play time—an A-like response?

2. to announce that you refuse to do the job your sons promised to do and that unless they do them, the pets have to go—a B-like response?

3. remember that you tend to respond on the stuck-in-needs-of-others (A) end of the graph, and consider a different tactic, one more towards the middle?

When we follow our habit of being stuck in the needs of others by continuing to feed the pets ourselves, we will probably feel used, resentful, and angry. These feelings come out when we least expect them and are rarely supportive of healthy relationships. If we choose to deliver an ultimatum—a more stuck-in-the-needs-of-self approach—we may end up having to take an action we would rather not take, i.e. getting rid of a turtle, two bunnies, and a puppy.

From the middle ground, we have many more options:

1. We can talk as a family about our pets, their needs, and our needs. Perhaps the tasks are too numerous for our sons to carry out every day because of their ages. Together we can make feeding, walking, grooming, and clean-up schedules that do not overly burden any of us.

2. Perhaps four pets are too many for our family to properly care for, and a neighbor would love one of the bunnies. Or the third grade class at our sons' school is studying reptiles and wants our turtle, except on the weekends when he can visit us.

3. Maybe the pets' homes, food, and water dishes need to be better organized to make caretaking easier, i.e. self-feeders, larger water containers, and so on.

Finding a middle ground between overgiving and overreceiving lets family members—including ourselves—breathe a sigh of relief. Kids think, "Oh, thank goodness, Mom and Dad do understand. They realized this job is too big for me, and I need help." Parents think, "Thank goodness I slowed myself down, carefully picked my way through this maze, recognized that hole I used to fall into, and found a way to keep everything from blowing up in my face!" FamilyMind thinking ensures that the needs of *all* family members are considered. The following checklist is helpful to refer to when we sense we may be getting close to falling into a deep hole in the sidewalk.

Checklist

1) Recognize the red flags.
   ❑ Red flags are those little warning signs that something is amiss in our relationships. They may be as subtle as a feeling of tension in the air, a sudden silence, or jokes and sarcasm directed at us. They may be as blatant as outright refusal to participate, verbal disagreements, or temper tantrums.

2) Acknowledge to yourself that something is off and tune in to the feeling messengers.

❑ I feel angry, unappreciated, used, and so on.

❑ The kids or my spouse seem upset.

❑ Someone (might be me) is delivering a lecture or a monologue.

3) Remember where on the give'ntake graph you tend to habitually react.

❑ Do I usually consider others to the exclusion of myself?

❑ Do I usually think of myself first and get lost in my own little world?

4) Consider what feelings are outside your feeling box and the behaviors you use to keep them there.

❑ Am I hiding anger behind tears?

❑ Am I afraid to ask for help when I need it?

❑ Do I talk all the time and refuse to listen to anyone else?

5) Check inside and ask these questions:

❑ What do I need?

❑ What do they need?

❑ Can I consider both right now, and what do I need to do?

6) Shift into FamilyMind thinking.

❑ Make a comment about what is happening in the moment: "Boy, we all seem upset right now." Or "We're sure quiet all of a sudden." Or "Did I do something?" Or "Ouch! That joke hurt my feelings. Are you bugged about something?"

❑ Or with younger children having a temper tantrum, sweep them up in your arms and say, "You're really upset. Let Daddy hold you."

7) Make necessary adjustments in behavior.

❑ Slow down.

❑ Speed up.

❑ Say more.

❑ Ask for more.

❑ Listen better.

And so on.

Next Step Summary:
How I Get Into the Hole

Now is the time to specifically identify the feeling messengers and/or personal preferences (likes/dislikes) you habitually ignore that make you fall into the hole of being disconnected from your soul and the real happenings that are going on around you.

Here are some examples:

How I fall in
When I get scared, I fall in the hole by detaching from my emotions, and that keeps me closed off from my soul and my family.

How I get out
I get out by tuning in to what I genuinely like and dislike about this situation, talk about it, and act on it.

How I fall in
When my husband is angry at me, I cringe and want to run away.

How I get out
I remember that anger was not allowed in my family of origin, and I know now that his anger means that something is very important to him and I seek to understand what that is.

How I fall in
I feel like crying, and I don't want to do anything.

How I get out
I check in with the feeling messenger of grief, and I realize that I have lost something important, and need to find out what that is, and how it now effects me.

How I fall in
Everyone in my family seems to be angry at me. I keep trying to get them organized, but things go from bad to worse.

How I get out
I remember that I tend to operate at the overreceiving end of the

give'ntake scale, and I adjust by inquiring into the real needs of others, and include my own.

Chapter Four
I walk down the same street.
There is a deep hole in the sidewalk.
I walk around it.[6]

A long time ago there ruled an Emperor who loved new clothes. All of his attention, time, and money from his treasury went into the pursuit of finer and richer attire. From morning to night he could be found in his dressing room, trying on the latest fashions. The Emperor's fancy for new clothes was known far and wide, and one day two strangers came to town claiming to be weavers. They described a marvelous cloth to the Emperor, so fine and so splendid that it was invisible to those who were incapable of doing their jobs properly, or who were unforgivably stupid. The Emperor thought that a new set of clothes made from such cloth could help him know which of his ministers were fit to serve him. He agreed to pay the strangers who set to work at once, feverishly working the threadless loom day and night. The townspeople murmured among themselves about the magical cloth. Many days passed. Unable to wait any longer, the Emperor sent his First Minister to see the new cloth and to report back about its exquisite colors and textures. To the First Minister's great alarm, he saw nothing on the loom. Afraid to let anyone know that he might be unsuited to hold his important office or that he might be terribly stupid, he told the Emperor how truly marvelous the new cloth was. How this pleased the Emperor.

Finally, the new clothes were finished, and to celebrate the occasion, the Emperor announced a parade for all to come to marvel at his newest, finest apparel. The Emperor hurried excitedly to his dressing room, but to his dismay, saw nothing in the hands of his would-be tailors. "Oh, dear," he said to himself, "Does this mean that I am not fit to be Emperor? I must let no one know!" So he donned his invisible finery and strode proudly down the street. His people shouted and exclaimed, "Oh, the lovely colors!" "Such intricate workmanship!" "Surely the finest clothes in his wardrobe!" Suddenly, the voice of a small boy was heard distinctly over the noise of the crowd, "But, he has nothing on!" he cried. After an uncomfortable silence the crowd then echoed the boy's revelation, "But, he has nothing on!" "The Emperor has nothing on!" The Emperor was relieved for surely the people were right. He thought to himself, "However, I must go on with the parade," and he marched grandly back to the palace with nothing on at all.[7]

—Hans Christian Andersen,
The Emperor's New Clothes

As children, there were times when our lives depended upon our trying to please our parents by pretending to be someone we were not. Many times our adopted behaviors saved us from punishment, embarrassment, or ridicule. As adults we continue to believe in the power of these behaviors, and we no longer know for sure who we are. We keep up the illusion for many reasons: it works; it is easier; it seems to make others happy; it is what we know how to do; it is how we survived; and most importantly, it's a habit. In the present we continue to use a behavior adopted in the past. Eventually, it becomes the "hole in our sidewalk," a deception, because we keep falling into the old routine, we forget how we got there, and we cannot see a way out.

No one was allowed to express anger in my family until it leaked out, and then anyone was fair game. All the anger we'd stored up came rushing out. In my marriage, the same thing used to happen. My wife would get angry at me for something, and I'd get angry back at her about something else. She kept complaining that I "piggybacked" on her anger. My therapist eventually helped me realize that when I brought up my own feelings when she was angry, I didn't have her full attention, and she didn't have mine. No wonder these outbursts went nowhere. I learned to bring up my own angry feelings during calm periods, so I had my wife's complete attention. She says she feels listened to, now that I don't have so much stored up inside and can give her time for her feelings. Now when my wife is angry, I think, "Oh, she's angry. This must be important." And I ask her to tell me more. It's funny, but we both seem less angry about everything.

—Jeff, forty-four

My home was not a very safe place to be when I was little. Whenever I felt scared or out of control, I used to tidy up the house. I put loose papers into piles, hid little odds and ends in drawers, emptied waste baskets, anything that would bring outside order to the inner chaos I felt. This annoyed my family members then, because they couldn't find anything when I was finished. It later annoyed my husband, because I had perfectionist standards of neatness he had trouble living up to. In therapy, I discovered that when I'm scared, I create safety by cleaning house. Now, if I need to clean the house and it's not dirty, I stop and ask myself, "What do I really need right now?" If I search back for what triggered my behavior, I often find that I'm scared. "Oh, my husband yelled at me this morning," I'll think to myself, remembering that yelling wasn't allowed in my family. Rather than cleaning house, I decide to tell my husband that I feel scared when he yells. Now I feel empowered, no longer small, scared, and helpless.

—Nola, thirty-seven

I thought if my family had a need, I was responsible for meeting it. I have this long list of things people want done that I said I would do, because I thought I should. Because I don't really want to do them, I procrastinate like crazy. Some of the things have been on the list for years, like repairing the gutters, fixing a screen door, and cleaning out the basement. When I was little, I wasn't allowed to say "No," when I didn't want to do something, and I realized that my mom did the same thing I do now. She could never say no to bake sales, school committees, and my dad's demands around the house. Like her, I shoulder every request anyone makes. After looking at an empty socket in the bathroom for a week, my wife finally blew up at me. I said, "I guess I have to learn to do things quicker." My wife replied, "No. That's not it at all! I'm angry because you said you'd get the bulb but didn't. If you weren't really going to get the bulb, I wish you'd said that no, you were sorry, but you didn't have time. I just mentioned we needed a bulb. I didn't mean you were the one who had to get it." That was an eye-opener for me. She wouldn't be mad at me if I said I couldn't do something!

—Mitchell, thirty-seven

I'm the kind of person who gets busier the busier my life gets. Rather than slowing down when things pile up on me, I take on more and more tasks. When I was young, I thought that if I just kept busy enough my dad wouldn't notice me, and I wouldn't keep getting on his bad side. I didn't realize then that there was nothing I could do to keep an alcoholic father from turning on me when he was drinking. Now in my adult life, I've realized that getting busier just makes people mad at me. When I start re-arranging the desktop on my computer, that's the sign for me that I need a break.

—Dennis, thirty-four

Reminder: The truly remarkable ability of the human psyche to adopt coping behaviors enables most of us to capably survive our childhood traumas. Even in the best of situations, the experiences life deals us demand we fit ourselves into society's mold. When we do not fit, we cut off parts of ourselves, as Procrustes, the evil marauder who attacked travelers on the road to ancient Athens did. "He had an iron bedstead, on which he used to tie all travelers who fell into his hands. If they were shorter than the bed, he stretched their limbs to make them fit it; if they were longer than the bed, he lopped off a portion." [8] We either stretch ourselves or cut off parts of ourselves for a purpose; our adopted behaviors and feelings helped us to meet a need in our childhoods. When an old behavior or feeling threatens to engulf us in a deep, dark hole, we must look for the original purpose of the old behavior. Then we must ask ourselves, "What do I *really* need *right now*? What does this family need right now, including me?" Once our new behaviors stop being new and become more familiar, we will discover a new way of living.

I no longer need to cry when I feel angry, like I did as a child.
Now I can express my anger in words when I feel angry, because I am an adult.

I no longer need to clean house when I am scared, like I did as a child.
Now I can check inside myself to see what's bothering me when I feel scared, because I am an adult.

I no longer need to blame others when I feel hurt, like I did as a child.
Now I can cry and talk about my pain when I feel hurt, because I am an adult.

I no longer yell when I feel helpless, like I did as a child
Now I can explain what I need and ask for help, because I am an adult.

I no longer need to overeat on sweets when I feel anxious, like I did as a child.

Now I can ask myself what I really need when I feel anxious, because I am an adult.

I no longer need to think only about the needs of others when I feel pressured, like I did as a child.

Now I can include my own needs, too, when I feel pressured, because I am an adult.

I no longer _____,
    like I did as a child.
Now I can _____,
    because I am an adult.

I no longer _____,
    like I did as a child.
Now I can _____,
    because I am an adult.

Chapter Five

I walk down another street. [9]

Once there was a wise man named Zuesa, who knew that the foundation for any community is built on how well it takes care of the poor, the elderly, the sick, and the young. So Zuesa went to the top of the mountain to seek guidance for how he could better serve his people. When he came down from the mountain, he was terrified. The people gathered around him and asked, "Zuesa, why are you so afraid?" He replied, "I now know what the angels will ask me on the last day." "But," the people protested, "You have led a model life." Zuesa said, "They're not going to ask me why, like Moses, I didn't take my people out of the promised land, and they're not going to ask me why, like Joshua, I didn't rescue my people from slavery."

"Zuesa," the people questioned, "What are they going to ask you?" Solemnly Zuesa replied, "They're going to ask me, 'Zuesa, why weren't you Zuesa?'" [10]

—an adaptation of a story told by Angeles Arrien,
Gathering Medicine

We cannot live the life of Moses, Joshua, or Zuesa, or by our spouse's or parents' expectations for us. We cannot follow the dogmas, beliefs, or values of others, nor can we continue to respond unconsciously to life's challenges. Walking down another street means living our lives fully from the daily promptings, preferences, and deep genuine desires of our souls. Continually asking, "Why aren't you Zuesa, or Mary, or Jack, or Denise, or John?" brings us back to the original intent or purpose behind our behaviors. What do I do that keeps me from being who I truly am? Why do I always cry when I am angry? What purpose did that behavior serve when I was young? How would I rather respond now? What behavior would better meet my needs today? What do I need right now?

Walking down a different street takes a willingness to listen to what is inside us and the courage to respond from our own sense of self and rightness. Walking down another street means listening to the voice of God within us. Theologian Carlye Marney gives a different interpretation to the story of Elijah (1 Kings 19:12 RSV) when he went to the mountain top to seek guidance from God. The scriptures say there was an earthquake, a fire, and a storm, and then Elijah heard a "still, small voice." Marney accuses the early translators of protecting us from the truth about what Elijah heard, because "still, small voice" in Hebrew means "utter silence." [11] How could we live with the thought that God did not answer Elijah, that He was silent? Elijah had to go into the silence of his own heart; he had to follow the promptings of his soul. From there we learn to live the only life worth living, our own.

Learning to walk down a different street does not mean we will now blissfully live our lives free of conflict. There are no perfect families where everyone's needs are always seen, understood, and championed. Our children will still develop patterns of behavior that help them survive in childhood but may hinder them as adults. We parents will still find ourselves unconsciously playing out old scenes from our childhoods. This is the remarkable, coping nature of the human being. Walking down a new street means we are willing and able to form new habits. Walking down a new street means we have shifted from being fascinated by the hole to being fascinated and committed to the journey of discovering our genuine needs and desires. They are the truest expressions of who we are.

Autobiography in Five Short Chapters

from *There's A Hole in My Sidewalk*
by Portia Nelson

Chapter One

I walk down the street.
There is a deep hole in the sidewalk.
I fall in.
I am lost....I am helpless.
It isn't my fault.
It takes forever to find a way out.

Chapter Two

I walk down the same street.
There is a deep hole in the sidewalk.
I pretend I don't see it.
I fall in again.
I can't believe I am in this same place.
But, it isn't my fault.
It still takes a long time to get out.

Chapter Three

I walk down the same street.
There is a deep hole in the sidewalk.
I see it is there.
I still fall in... it's a habit... but,
my eyes are open.
I know where I am.
It is my fault.
I get out immediately.

Chapter Four

I walk down the same street.
There is a deep hole in the sidewalk.
I walk around it.

Chapter Five

I walk down another street.[12]

Endnotes: Part Five

1. Portia Nelson, *There's a Hole in My Sidewalk: The Romance of Self-Discovery* (Hillsboro, OR: Beyond Words, 1993), 2.

2. Ibid.

3. Ibid., 3.

4. Walt Kelly, 1970 *Pogo* cartoon used in 1971 Earth Day poster.

5. Michael Mayer, *The Mystery of Personal Identity* (San Diego, CA: ACS Publications, 1984), 7.

6. Nelson, *There's a Hole*, 3.

7. Hans Christian Andersen, "Story of the Emperor's New Clothes," as told in The Yellow Fairy Book, Andrew Lang ed. (New York: Dover, 1966), 21-25.

8. Thomas Bulfinch, *The Age of Fable* (New York: New American Library, 1962), 189.

9. Nelson, *There's a Hole*, 3.

10. Angeles Arrien, *Gathering Medicine: Stories, Songs, and Methods for Soul-Retrieval*, audiocassette produced by Sounds True Recordings, Boulder, CO, 1994, Part Two.

11. Carlye Marney, *Priests To Each Other* (Valley Forge, PA: Judson Press, 1974), 69.

12. Nelson, *There's a Hole*, 2-3.

PART SIX

Conflict: An Opportunity for Intimacy

The sword cannot build relationships:
it can't settle anything, it can't bind together.
It can only rip apart.
If you want to heal your relationship, build
relationship, then you must learn to use
the language of the harp.
You must affirm the other person,
express your love and feeling and devotion.
This is an absolute law:
The harp heals and binds together;
the sword wounds and cuts asunder.[1]

—Robert Johnson,
We: Understanding the Psychology of Romantic Love

Conflict is a natural part of life. Conflict happens no matter what we do to try to avoid it. Someone leaves their snack dishes in the family room—again—and we find a long trail of ants the next morning. We feel frustrated. While balancing the checkbook, Mom discovers that Dad forgot to record several cash withdrawals last month. She feels scared. Our daughter is worried about an upcoming speech for school. In her nervousness, she comes to dinner short-tempered and says something mean about the meal.

We feel hurt. Everyone has their own scenarios, and the lists go on and on.

Life will never be free of conflict. Conflict is not the problem. *How we feel about conflict and how we respond to conflict is what matters.* Understanding conflict as an opportunity to get to know family members better, and to become closer to them as a result of seeing the conflict through, allows us to respond more authentically to everyday family interactions. When we know that conflict is a normal part of family life, *and that we can work it out,* we don't have to walk on egg shells, afraid to say what we really feel. Many of us learned to hide certain parts of ourselves from our parents to keep the peace or avoid disapproval or punishment. To avoid conflict, we kept some of our true feelings shut away, boxed in, to be safe. The sad legacy of hiding feelings is that family members fail to really know each other, to develop a level of intimacy that touches each of our souls, to give each person a true feeling of belonging.

Learning to avoid the holes in our sidewalks and walk down new streets does not necessarily mean conflict-free living. Using Family-Mind thinking at home does not guarantee that we will never butt heads with our mates or our children, because when we consider the differing needs between individuals, between genders, and between children and adults, it is a wonder family members ever get along at all! Understanding these need differences helps us deal with them, but we must also learn to use the appropriate language for the situations we find ourselves in.

Sword Language

We all have a natural "fight or flight" instinct towards conflict. We flee from it by ignoring it, denying it, or running from it. We fight it by standing our ground and slugging it out. If we respond to conflict with the sword, as Robert Johnson, author and Jungian analyst, describes it, we create chaos and separation, because the language of the sword is cutting, rational, and swift. It divides and conquers, leaving no room for the sharing of feelings, understanding another's viewpoint, or coming to compromises. If we consistently use the sword, we get worn down by the vicious cycle of conflict: skirmish, angry words or actions, feelings of blame, loneliness, isolation, and the desire to leave. Although the language of the sword is useful in the workplace, where the analyzing intellect is needed to cut through piles of information for decision-making, it can be a destructive force in the home. Dr. Johnson asserts, "We often hear a man and woman trying to 'settle things' by arguing, criticizing each other, talking logic, poking holes in each other's arguments, splitting hairs. Then they wonder why all the spontaneous feeling of love and warmth has gone out of their marriage or their time together!"[2]

Harp Language

The language of the harp, however, allows time to let feelings come up, provides room to discover what one truly likes and dislikes, lets us check to see what old habit is getting in the way, and clarifies what we all really, really need. The harp slows us down, helps us listen to each other, shows us the positive intent beneath our words and actions, and brings us toward understanding, belonging, and harmony. The harp connects us to our souls, wherein lies our deepest needs, wants, and wishes.

The soul speaks the language of the harp, the home of the heart life. Our passions, talents, and resources lie within our souls. In children these soul forces are alive and often stronger than the child is. This can make some children extremely difficult to live with.

> From infancy my daughter always knew what she wanted, and it was usually the opposite of what she was offered. If I gave her fruit, she wanted meat; if I gave her meat, she wanted vegetables. When her dad tried to comfort her with walking, she wanted rocking. If we gave her the blue ball, she wanted the red one. She was always frustrated, and so were we! Now, at thirty-one, Sheila is a fashion designer with several apprentices under her. She knows her style, and she deftly weeds out any imperfections or mismatches. I've never seen anyone so sure of herself, and she loves her work.
>
> —Gina, sixty-five

True communication and belonging in a family comes from the soul force that speaks the language of the harp. It is the secret of Family-Mind thinking. When we pause long enough to hear the soul speaking in our mates, our children, and ourselves we have touched the solution to conflict. Asking, "Is this what we want to be doing right now?" and, "What does this family need right now, including me?" brings us to the core of human experience, the soul. At the soul level lie the vital ingredients that unite us and create life and vitality within the family.

My wife, Jenny, and I have been married for twenty-one years. After all this time, we rarely have a conversation that doesn't end in an argument or a standoff. But, we get by, our kids are great, we both work hard, and we make a good living, so we've managed to stay together. My biggest frustration is that Jenny often says she wants more passion in our lives, so I give her special gifts, surprise trips alone, and romantic get-aways together, but no matter what I do, I never seem to please her.

I finally agreed to counseling, because I had tried everything else to please Jenny. During our first session, the therapist listened for a few minutes, then turned to my wife and said, "What you want most from Jerry is to be able to talk with him about your passions—what has real meaning to you in your life." She looked surprised for a minute and then quietly said, "Yes! I want to tell him about my love and passion for my sculpting. I want to take long walks with him, to share with him about my dreams, struggles, and personal ambitions for my work. I want him to understand my joys and my agonies." I sat in shocked silence, but what Jenny said next, surprised me even more. "All those special things you've done for me over the years have been nice. What I'd love most would be for you to tell me about your greatest passions and dreams, too. I want to know what you long for, how you really want to live your life, what we can do together to make things better for each of us." "That's all you want?" I asked, amazed. I had no clue it was something so simple. Although I wasn't used to talking about those deep things, and it was hard at first, I realized that I had been longing for someone to want to know about me, to understand how I see the world. My heart hurt the first time I told Jenny about some difficult times in my childhood, but to have her know what I had suffered made me able to trust her more and be more affectionate and emotionally open.

—Jerry, forty-six

Jenny wanted her husband, Jerry, to see her soul—her preferences, passions, and hatreds. On a very deep level she longed for him to empathize with what she felt about her experiences, about her artwork, about life. She wanted to connect with him on that soul level, too. The tragic childhood experience of losing his father caused Jerry to hide his deepest thoughts and feelings under the cover of a sharp wit and shrewd intellect. Have a problem or complaint? Jerry's the man. Jerry's habitual response—jumping in too soon with his own opinions or solutions—shattered the connection Jenny tried to make with him by sharing her thoughts and feelings.

This story also illustrates some of the differences in communication styles between men and women. Deborah Tannen, Ph.D., linguist, scholar, and author, found that men tend to use communication to get things done and to maintain status—a sword language. Women are more apt to use communication to establish rapport and to maintain connection—the language of the harp.[3] When Jerry understood what Jenny needed—to share her soul's desire—he was willing to work on being a better listener. Jenny also realized she had to change her way of asking for help, understanding that Jerry needed clear, short, and direct explanations when being asked for something. When they fight now, they have ways to get back to listening to each other, rather than escalating into ways that separate and divide them.

Using the language of the harp does not mean, necessarily, that the words we use to describe our troubles are beautiful. They may come out in angry, ragged barbs, aimed to hurt. Our frustration or rage may be so great that we rant on and on until the storm has passed, leaving pain and wreckage in our wake. In her fascinating work on families called, *Intimate Worlds: Life Inside the Family*, researcher and writer Maggie Scarf discovers that within workable, intimate families, each member's expression of negative feelings, such as despair, discouragement, anger, frustration, and sadness, is considered a birthright. "In these families, angry feelings and sad feelings are thus not merely 'allowed' or 'permitted'; they are *expected* [our italics] to exist, welcomed, and even embraced as aspects of a loved family member's own unique humanity."[4] These families have become adept at using harp language to resolve the inevitable conflict of living together and growing into full human beings.

Unfortunately, many of us come from families that believed in the Cinderella myth. Once the Prince and Cinderella find each other, they live the rest of their lives without conflict. We expect to grow up, have a satisfying career, meet Prince Charming or Sleeping Beauty, have one point five children, and live happily ever after. When we have the right job, meet the right partner, have the right clothes, reach the right weight, have the right house, car, stereo, computer, and so on, we will be happy. And happiness in this story means *no conflicts*—no bad moods, failures, arguments, disagreements, disappointments, or divorces. We believe if we suffer these conflicts, our relationship is bad, our mate is the wrong person, our children are rotten, we have failed, and we have to leave. In fact, all these conflicts are opportunities for discovering the real needs of the people involved. The bigger the conflict, the more important the needs, and the more skills we must use to find out what is beneath all the trouble.

Welcoming Conflict

Within a family, communication is affected by many factors: gender, age, role responsibilities, financial responsibilities, temperament, parents' families of origin, habits, values, and so on. *The purpose of communication within the family is to help each other find who we are through what we really need and give support in living it.* This communication uses the language of the harp. The following conflict resolution guidelines open the way for living in FamilyMind by nurturing the soul of a family.

Listen for the Positive Intent. A small child crying in the supermarket is often tired and hungry. Beneath his tears is the message, "I need your help. Please take me home; I cannot control myself any longer." The angry teen who yells, "I hate you!" is trying desperately to make contact and to tell us that she needs us. A frustrated husband who slams the door and stomps out into the night may be saying to his wife, "I need to protect myself by leaving when you criticize me." Although the words and behaviors seem negative to us, they all carry an underlying meaning we call the *positive intent.* All three people in the previous examples are metaphorically "waving a red flag" to say, "Hey! Something is important here! I have strong feelings about this! Please listen. Please care. Please help me!" Each of these conflictual situations provides an opportunity for increased understanding and connection with another person. By hearing the positive intent in our toddler's screams, we can scoop him out of the grocery cart and lovingly say, "Oh, you've been helping me shop for so long; I'm tired, too. Let's go home." Temper tantrums are always embarrassing, and leaving before we have all the groceries is a great imposition, but imagine what it would have been like if your own parents had understood your need without punishing, shaming, or blaming you, because they were embarrassed by your bad behavior. By listening for the positive intent beneath our little one's screams, we welcome his feelings, whatever they are; we show him compassion; we gain his trust; and we teach him that he is more important than the groceries. In turn, he learns to listen to his own feelings and will eventually be able to tell us in words, rather than in tantrums, what he needs. We can compensate by making sure he is fresh and full when we go to the store; by realizing the store is too overwhelming for him at his age and arrange for him to stay home with Dad when we shop; or by asking Dad or someone else to go to the store for us. Looking at what our family needs by listening to the positive intent frees us to find alternatives that work for everyone.

Most of us can probably think of many things we would rather do than go to the supermarket with a toddler, screaming or otherwise!

> *It took me awhile to understand the positive intent idea. When my wife criticized me, I always got angry. "How can she treat me this way?" I'd think. I took her comments personally, as though she were my moral judge, or something. When I learned that her criticism signaled that she was upset about something, I could back off, ask her to tell me more about what I did or didn't do that bothered her, and try to understand. Most of the time, I was trying to do too many things at once and not really getting anything finished. Never completing tasks was something her dad did, and she explained it made her feel insecure, that everything might fly out of control. The positive message underneath her criticism was, "Help! Slow down. I'm feeling nervous and scared." Well, I could respond easily to that!*

> —*Jasper, thirty*

There is always an underlying meaning—a positive intent—to our words and behaviors. No matter the content, our communication with others carries an unspoken message from our souls—the *positive intent*. Listening for the positive intent of a family member's words or actions often prevents misunderstandings and arguments from erupting. Listening for the positive intent opens the way for understanding between two people, rather than creating the escalating arguments that usually fall on four deaf ears!

We communicate with others to meet a need, want, or wish, or to solve a problem. Under pressure, we often say things we do not mean, use words that do not accurately describe what we want to say, or use words as a shield to protect our vulnerabilities. Rather than getting the results we want, our words hide our true motives. When we shout, "You *never* do *anything* around the house!" we are really saying, "I feel overwhelmed. There's too much to do. I'm under too much pressure. I need your help." For various reasons, our attempt to solve a problem, or ask for what we need, comes out in a clumsy, sometimes blaming, way.

Trust invites openness. Many of us do not feel safe in our families to expose our needs, wants, and wishes. Long experience of not being understood, yelled at, ridiculed, and blamed makes us shy about sharing our genuine feelings. It may be easier to accuse, "You *never* do *anything* around the house!" than it is to reveal, "I need your help. I can't do it all alone." When family members listen for the positive intent behind each others' words and behaviors, we develop a trust that we are cared about, that we are important, that others want to know our deepest selves.

Listening for the positive intent allows us to "count from one to ten." When someone accuses us of doing or not doing something, many of us instinctively jump on the other side of the line and, figuratively speaking, put up our fists. Our immediately defensive stance sets up an adversarial situation. By pausing to look for the positive intent behind words or behaviors, we can step out of the line of fire for a moment and focus the attention upon the other person, rather than working out a defense tactic to protect ourselves.

Naming the positive intent is the first step in a behavioral change. When we help name the intent beneath someone's words, she or he feels seen and heard. Usually, the person is then able to step back from an accusing stance and express his or her needs so that we can hear them without needing to be on the defensive. Knowing the positive intent only gets us halfway there. Without action or follow through, it is merely an intellectual exercise. If our son says, "I didn't *mean* to leave my lunch dishes on the table," and we understand that his intent was to put them in the dishwasher, but he proceeds to leave them, nothing has been accomplished. When we are helped to see what we really want to say, we must then engage our wills toward positive, loving action. All family members are called upon to change their behaviors in the face of a positive intent. Whether we must learn to listen more deeply before responding, to communicate our feelings more directly, or to stop making agreements we cannot keep, loving action is the desired result of our efforts to understand one another.

Hearing the Positive Intent

The following are common statements and behaviors with their hidden positive intent.

Statement or Behavior	Positive Intent
Toddler tantrum at the grocery store.	I'm tired. I'm hungry.
"You never listen to me."	I value your company. I need your input.
"I hate this house!"	I need more space, beauty, order.
"You never let me do anything."	I want you to trust me.
"I'm not your maid!"	I feel taken advantage of.
"You never do anything around the house!"	I'm overwhelmed. I need your help. I'm under too much pressure.
"Why can't you remember to do anything I ask you to do?"	I feel left alone with all the work. Let's work together.
"You're stupid!"	I feel misunderstood.
Son breaks window and denies it.	I'm afraid of your anger. I don't know what to do. I need your guidance.

To answer the FamilyMind Question, **"What does this family need now, including me?"** we must be in touch with our own and others' needs. To hear and understand the language of the soul, we heed our feeling messages, and we listen for the positive intent behind words and behaviors.

Positioning is sword action and sets up an "us vs. them" way of thinking. When we enter a discussion or conversation with definite and inflexible expectations about how things should or will come out, we have taken a position. Positioning brings about a win-lose or lose-lose situation; puts people on the defensive; works on assumptions that may be false; isolates the participants; and eliminates choices. Positioning is easily seen in the workplace: The employee says to the boss, "I want a raise." The boss replies, "You can't have one." The employee says, "Then I'll go on strike until I get one." The Boss says, "I'll hire someone to take your place." The employee counters, "I'll get the union to strike your whole company." The boss comes back, "We'll hire all new people." The employee says, "We'll shut down your office everyday." The boss replies, "We are bigger than you and can wait you out." This position-based interaction goes on and on, escalating with each interchange. Without intending it, and before we know it, total war is declared.

This scenario happens at home just as easily and is just as deadly. One parent takes the position that television is bad for the whole family and wants to get rid of it. The other parent supports supervised viewing for entertainment and education. In this interchange one parent can be viewed as rigid and mean, while the other can be considered uncaring and uninformed. The different sides face off, and the battle is on. An argument about how much one does or doesn't do around the house can escalate into a hurtful contest about "I do more than you do," and "You're lazy and I'm not!" The one who feels criticized will fight to the death. One parent thinks the children should see only PG movies, and the other thinks that a PG-13 movie with an important message is okay for their young teenager. One is seen as protective of the children's tender sensibilities, while the other doesn't seem to care what the children are exposed to. Both parents dig in their heels and refuse to budge from their superior positions. The teenager, desperately wanting to go to the concert with the gang and knows his parents will oppose it, sees himself as a wronged innocent and his parents as the mean jailers even before he broaches the subject. With this setup, his plea is doomed to fail. A discussion between intimates about their sexual life can turn the position of "I want more sex" into "You are a sexual pervert." Or, "Well, you're a cold prude!" Such a standoff can last for weeks.

> *Out beyond ideas of wrong doing and right doing,*
>
> *there's a field, I'll meet you there.*[5]

—Rumi, thirteenth century Persian poet

When we come to the bargaining table or the courtroom we have a position to defend. When we attempt to listen to the needs of our family members, or to voice our own, an attitude of hopeful openness is more beneficial. In families where feelings and needs are seen as a natural part of who we are, members are less likely to use positioning. Because needs are valued and listened to, we don't have to engage our armory of weapons for an all-out defensive; we remain connected to those involved; we check out our assumptions or voice our fears; and many choices open up before us. In this need-based interaction, we focus on the *interests* of all the parties, rather than on the *positions* of all the parties. The boss asks the employee for more information and discovers that a new baby is on the way or that the wife has a serious illness. Now the issue of the raise takes on a new perspective. Perhaps more information is needed about the company's health coverage, a bonus is due, or a raise can be negotiated. With the *needs* clearly stated, the boss and employee can approach the problem from the same side, rather than as adversaries defending their separate positions. When approached from the same side, the argument between spouses about household chores could be clarified from the start with the questions, "What am I not doing that upsets you so?" From a parenting partnership perspective, issues about television and movie watching can be resolved from a caring, need-based interaction. The special needs of teens to do some things independently from the family require careful listening, patient negotiating, and balanced give'ntake from *everyone* involved. Intimate conversations about sexual needs and desires call for tender understanding and mutual sharing to create a relationship that is mutually satisfying.

I'm a work-at-home-mom, and my husband works in the city. Every vacation, it's the same thing—I do all the planning, all the packing, all the shopping, all the last minute details that have to be done so we can be gone for two weeks, arrange for a house sitter, stop the mail, let the relatives know, and so on. Stan crams a week's worth of work into two days, so we can leave on a Wednesday to beat the weekend traffic, and we don't see him for two days! By the time we are ready, I'm exhausted and mad! It's no fun doing everything by yourself, and cleaning and unpacking when we get home, too.

—Trish, thirty-seven

The husband's position in the previous scenario is, "I have to work for the money." The wife's position is, "It's not fair that I have to work alone before, during, and after our vacation. That is not a vacation for me." When Trish and Stan discuss their vacation issues from a position-based stance, they both become defensive and stuck. "You're never around to help me get ready!" "I'm working to earn the money to *go* on vacation!" "You do this *all* the time." "There's nothing else I *can* do." And so on, until both Trish and Stan feel resentful, blamed, unheard, unappreciated, and alone.

Let us look at their exchange from a need-based discussion. "I need help getting ready. It's too much to do alone." "I need to go to the office on Monday and Tuesday." With their needs out in open, this couple decided to leave on Thursday, using Wednesday as a day to work together on getting ready to go. Trish left more relaxed and Stan felt more included in the family's vacation preparations. Taking positions leaves us little flexibility for meeting the swiftly changing needs of family life. FamilyMind living allows us to focus on the needs of the moment, to learn more about each other, to stay connected, and to make decisions that benefit the whole family.

Practice using need-based responses to your family life situations. Here are some examples:

Statement	Positioned Response	Need Response
I want a soda!	No. It's too close to dinner.	Oh, you need a drink.
You don't love me.	Of course, I love you!	What did I do that you don't like?
This kitchen's a mess.	I just cleaned it up!	What did I not do that upsets you?

Avoid *always* and *never*. Telling family members how their behavior affects us is crucial for loving relationships. These comments are most effective when we talk about current actions. Saying, "You **never** put your dirty dishes away," or "You **always** leave your dirty dishes out," immediately puts a daughter on the defensive for the many times she did put her snack dishes in the dishwasher. Before we know it, we're off in another power struggle, when all we actually wanted to do was let her know that, *today*, we were frustrated when she left her dishes for someone else to put away. Letting her know how we feel about *this* failure to act, opens the way for communication to occur: "**When you** leave your snack dishes on the counter, **I feel** taken for granted and hurt." Learning that our behavior has an effect on others is an important part of growing up. Being able to tell others how their behavior affects us *in a way they can hear* is an essential part of effective communication.

When a family member uses *always* or *never*, it helps to listen for the underlying positive intent of their message. Saying, "You *never* pick up after yourself!" to your husband, is a signal to him that this issue is important. Although he may bristle at the use of *never*, he can take it as a clue that you have strong feelings and need to be heard. His reminder that using *never* makes it difficult for him to hear your feelings helps to rephrase the complaint. "**When you** leave your clothes on the floor of the closet, **I feel** used like a maid." These honest feelings open the way for apology, compromise, or more discussion about the issue—whether it really needs to be done, how it could be done more consistently, and so on.

Do not use name-calling, stupid! Being labeled immediately gets our dander up. When we are on the defensive, it is impossible to hear anything more than the offensive name. How many times has one of our children come running home with wounded pride, crying, "He called me, 'Silly!'" No matter how often we respond with, "Don't pay any attention to him," or "Sticks and stones may break your bones, but words will never hurt you," the child is not comforted. Name-calling is a slander that goes deeply into the heart and stops us cold. We may feel indignant, shameful, or angry, and some of us want to withdraw where we can no longer be hurt.

⇦ *JEANNE* | In one of my communication classes, I was taught to label the behavior, not the person. I found, however, that when I said to Don, "You did something stupid," it had the same result as if I had called *him* stupid.

Name-calling inherently carries judgment, and judgment usually implies criticism. When we tell the truth without blame or judgment, we share how we responded to the behavior. Angeles Arrien, Ph.D., a powerful folklorist and teacher, relates the following story:

I was deeply touched several months ago, when I was waiting for the shuttle to take me to the airport. I was sitting next to a woman who was reading her newspaper, but my eyes were totally engrossed on a fourteen-year-old on his skateboard. He had his baseball cap turned around—you know, with the bill in back, the "cool" look? And he buzzed us once, and then he came around and buzzed us twice, and when he came around for the third, magnificent buzz, he inadvertently knocked the paper out of this woman's hands. And she said, "Oh, why don't you grow up!" And he went down to the corner to talk to his buddy. They talked, and they looked back at us, and then they talked some more, and then they looked back at us. In the meantime, she was rolling up her paper. She put it under her arm, and she stood up. She went to the middle of the block, and she motioned to him and said, "Won't you come here? I want to talk to you." So reluctantly and very slowly he came up on his skateboard, and he turned his cap around with the bill up in front, and said, "Yeah?" And she said, "What I meant to say was that I was afraid that I might get hurt. I apologize for what I did say." His face has been a source of inspiration for me all year long, because his face lit up, and he said, "How cool."[6]

—Angeles Arrien, *Gathering Medicine:*
Stories, Songs, and Methods for Soul-Retrieval

Use ten words or less for sons and fathers. Most males prefer communication short and to the point with the problem stated first, then the discussion. Men and boys hear an expression of feelings or a request when made clearly and directly. Otherwise, they hear only the problem and want to go immediately to the solution.

"Hang up your clothes now, please."

"When you yell, I feel scared."

"I'm tired. Let's go out to eat tonight."

"No, I do not want to hold your snake."

"Ummmm, rub my back again, right there. Ahhhh."

Of course, we are *not* saying that men and boys cannot carry on a conversation of more than ten words. When communicating how we feel about something, or when we need to ask that a task be done, many males get defensive, jump way ahead of us to a solution, or run out the door, if we go into a long lecture. Ten words or less say we know what we are talking about, or that we are clear about what we want. This can sometimes be a stretch for mothers and daughters, because they habitually use more words, but being brief, clear, and confident is reassuring to fathers and sons. It touches their souls.

Use three paragraphs with mothers and daughters. Connection and relationship are primary to most females, and verbal communication is their greatest medium. Taking time to assure the relationship is intact (paragraph one), to explain the problem (paragraph two), and to reaffirm that we can work it out (paragraph three), allows daughters and mothers to feel cared for and understood. Taking more time and using more words can be a stretch for fathers and sons, who prefer to be brief and concise, but is well worth the effort.

> *Before my husband understood my style of communicating, I often felt hurt and misunderstood when I shared my day with him. I would begin by telling what happened at the office with a workmate of mine, maybe complaining that she hadn't finished a project on time, expecting him to be sympathetic and understanding of my frustration and inconvenience. Instead, he would immediately say she should be fired, that someone lax like that shouldn't be allowed to keep her high-paying position, and on and on. My day got totally lost in his indignation about how people work, and that's not a problem with my workmate at all. Sometimes, I'd get so mad at him, I'd just stop talking altogether, and you can bet I'd go right to sleep that night, too!*

> —*Judy, forty-five*

Withholding causes separation and isolation. Refusing to "talk about it" and withdrawing affection are ways of the sword. These behaviors do nothing to foster connection and relationship. Some of us do need time away from the heat of the moment to pass through the nonthinking zone, count to ten, calm down, and re-enter the clear-thinking zone. However, saying, "I'm really upset right now, and I don't want to say something I'd be sorry about, so I need a time out," is different from refusing to talk at all. Spouting off, clamming up, and storming out cause others to feel afraid, angry, left out, abandoned, and defensive. Most people find it difficult to maintain a connection when they have these feelings.

Some of us need time alone to cool off and think about it before feeling ready to talk. Others recover quickly and want to duke it out right then and there. Understanding and respecting each family member's way of dealing with conflict helps get us through the rough places. This is not to say that we have to *like* how the others react to stress and disagreement. If a husband's way of dealing with disharmony is totally alien to our way, we may be soothed when we express how we feel. This is best done in a moment of quiet and harmony when listening and responding are optimum.

"I understand you need to calm down and think about this, but when you leave, I feel abandoned."

"When you insist we talk about it right in the moment, I feel trapped, pressured, and afraid I'll blow up and hurt you."

The previous examples use the language of the harp. We offer understanding, show care, and maintain connection by sharing how we feel. In these moments, conflict is transformed into an opportunity for opening more deeply to each other.

It is important to make a distinction between privacy and withholding or keeping secrets. We all need room for our own private thoughts and dreams, and we must not expect that family members share all their deepest ruminations with each other. Withholding secret information important to the connection and harmony of the group or to the safety of individual members, however, can be risky and hurtful. Hopefully, our children feel comfortable coming to us when they know a dangerous secret—Sister is sneaking out at night, Brother is using drugs, Sister is skipping school, and so on. Betraying a family member may seem shameful, but the costs to the family of keeping such secrets warrant this action.

Foster re-grouping. After an explosion in group harmony, families need to re-group. Re-grouping often happens naturally, like the symbol of the Tao; relations wax and then wane, we drift apart and come together, ebb and flow, in and out. Sometimes, parents must be what Angeles Arrien calls "shape-shifters,"[7] ones who can shift the shape of an encounter or situation.

With young children a story or song is often effective to dissolve the resulting tension. Perhaps a group hug brings everyone back to connection, or a joke or humorous story restores equilibrium. Be sure that re-grouping happens only after the conflict and the feelings surrounding it have been expressed and/or resolved. We humans find it quite difficult to feel connected while disagreements are alive and raw.

Whatever the conflict and the resolution, asking the FamilyMind Question, "What does this family need right now, including me?" gets everyone back on track.

Use "work-arounds" consciously. Work-arounds are behaviors that allow us to avoid dealing with current issues and the genuine needs of the group. Here is an example: The wife is angry when the husband continually comes home ten minutes late from work. Instead of discussing it, the guy drives like crazy to be on time, or he walks in, changes the subject, and offers to do extra things to help out. He is making a work-around; trying to avoid the conflict of why his wife is angry with him. He is taking a shortcut around what is really going on by using avoidance, diversion, and placating. By not dealing with her issues, he risks all kinds of other problems— speeding tickets, accidents, resentment, keeping score, misunderstandings, slip-ups at work, and so on. When difficulties begin to happen, we can be certain it is because there is something else going on.

> *My husband has a terrible temper, and I hate making him mad at me. The last time he was upset, I just left for work before he got up, so I didn't have to face him. I could only avoid him for so long, because we both started to feel guilty, but I carried it off for a couple of days.*
>
> *—Shirley, forty-nine*

Work-arounds are not necessarily bad. Conflicts can arise when we least expect them, usually at the most inopportune moments. If we have too much to deal with at the time, a work-around may be just what we need until we are free to respond without feeling overwhelmed. As Shirley says in the previous story, we can avoid it only so long, and then the wound begins to fester. The key to knowing whether a work-around is helpful is to decide whether we want to avoid something out of fear or out of need. If we habitually steer away from conflict because we fear the outcome or the person involved, our actions usually backfire on us—we have an accident, get confronted about our behavior, or goof up badly. Consciously choosing to work around a conflict works best when we tell those involved what we need.

"I know you're angry, but I'm so overwhelmed with problems at work right now. Could we talk about this tomorrow?"

"Your feelings are important to me, but I'm just too angry myself to hear you right now. I need a break."

"I'm sorry I can't listen right now, because I'm late, but I'll come home early rather than going out to eat, so we can talk."

Use direct requests, not "can you?" When we ask, "Can you do this for me?" we leave ourselves wide open for refusal or sarcasm. "Jimmy, can you take out the trash?" "Well, sure, Mom, I *can*, but I don't want to now." Asking "can you?" is really asking, "Are you able?" Most of us will reply, "Yes, we are able, but...." "Jimmy, please take out the trash," is clear, direct, and leaves no room for sarcasm or refusal. Most of us respond much better to this form of communication when the request is reasonable and timely.

Ask for support, not for permission. All family members need to ask each other for permission to use personal property. Young children ask their parents for permission for pretty much everything, and the need to ask decreases with age and maturity. Actually, family life is a constant series of negotiations and consultations. Between mates these interchanges are most effective when shared adult to adult. When a spouse asks for permission—for example, "Can I go out tonight?"—the asker is put in a childlike position and the receiver in a parental position. Neither role is effective in a negotiation, and the one asked will be resentful if s/he feels responsible for making the other's decision.

"Honey, I need a break, and Bob has two tickets to the game. I want to go. How would this affect you?" clearly states the facts. In this case, the husband says what he needs and asks his wife for support. Both persons maintain an equal ground and open the way for connection through communication. If the wife is unable to support his going out tonight, the husband can ask what must happen so he gets the break he needs, and a discussion flows from there. *The key in this interchange is that the husband asks for support, not permission, and remains unattached to the outcome.* Asking for permission invites resentment, because the wife feels angry for being put in the position of parent. The husband needs a break, but it may not come in the shape of going to the ball game. Being attached to how or when he gets a break provokes possible disappointment and resentment for him. The wife may need her husband home that evening. The children may need their father home that evening. The husband needs a break.

Asking, "What does this family need right now, including me?" helps begin the discussion. Dad needs a break so he can come back to the family group refreshed with renewed energy for listening, giving, and loving. Can the other needs be deferred or taken care of without Dad's being at home? All these needs and questions must be put in the family stew pot, simmered, stirred, and poured out to be understood and negotiated between partners, adult to adult. Remembering that the purpose of family communication is to foster relationships and support each others' growth, we look for solutions that help members maintain connection with each other by acknowledging and supporting genuine desires and needs.

Bring up angry issues when not angry. Many of us grew up in families where angry issues were rarely resolved, because most feelings were either denied or ignored. When the anger came out, it was often an open invitation for everyone to burst out with their withheld resentments, and caused an explosion. For most of us, anger was either shameful—it shouldn't happen—or dangerous— kaboooom!

Anger is valuable, especially in a family situation, because it is a raw and fresh expression of one's heart's desire—the genuine need. Learning to listen to each other's anger allows us to hear the heart's desire. Many of us, especially men, have a tendency to hold on to our angry feelings until someone else expresses theirs.

Wife: (Angrily) "You didn't say 'Good Morning' to me."

Husband: (Angry back) "Well, *you* didn't say 'Good Morning' to *me!*"

We can all imagine what happens next—this couple becomes hopelessly entangled in their anger.

We find the following solution very helpful: Let's say the wife brings up angry feelings. She gets to go first and has the floor. The husband listens for her heart's desire. At a later time, he can bring up his concerns, if necessary. It is very important to allow time to digest the discussion and get through the feelings evoked. Otherwise, the experience is like having one's sentence cut off in the middle by someone who couldn't wait to get his own ideas into the conversation. The same happens when the sharing of feelings, especially anger, is not given ample time and space. The angry one feels unfinished, unheard, and unsatisfied.

Use "Tell me more." When strong feelings are expressed, the best way to respond is, "Tell me more," because strong feelings signal, "This is important to me! This is my soul's desire speaking!" The following is an example of what happens when we respond to content, rather than listening for the positive intent or soul's desire beneath the words.

Husband: "I hate it when you don't have dinner ready when I get home, since you're not working anymore."

Wife: "What do you mean, since I'm not working? I work all the time. I get no respect for what I do!"

Husband: (Stomps out the door, feeling unheard and unseen.)

In this exchange, the wife got tangled up in content, "...you're not working...", and forgot to listen to the underlying message—her husband's soul's desire. The husband felt uncared for and thought, "I'm alone in my family, trying to live a life that isn't really mine. I can't go on living like this. I have to get away to be myself." He feels genuine sadness for himself and his predicament.

A FamilyMind response to the husband's feelings is, "Having dinner ready when you get home sounds really important to you. *Tell me more.*"

Husband: "I work hard, and I want to be cared for when I get home."

Wife: "Are you saying you don't feel cared about when you come home?"

Husband: "When my dad came home from work, my mom always had dinner on the table for him, and he knew she loved him."

The bottom line for this man was that he felt left out and uncared for when he came home. His expectations that his wife have dinner ready, because his mother always did, were not giving him what he most wanted—love and belonging. When the wife understood the issue, she explained that she was often too tired to fix dinner alone, because she had been caring for three small children all day. The husband understood this, and together they looked at their alternatives.

In these situations, it is helpful to examine our options, not our "have to's." Often our expectations about how something *should* happen is a "have to" from our childhood. This husband's mother always had dinner ready for his father; she had to so he felt loved. Without looking at other options, the husband insisted his wife have dinner ready, too. As it turned out, the couple in our example discovered they *both* wanted caring when the husband came home from work. They agreed to experiment to find what best met their needs. One night, they sat down together in the backyard and had tea, while the children played around them. Another night they cuddled on the sofa and told each other about their day; then they got dinner together. This husband now looks forward to coming home from work, because his soul desires are being met. His wife learned to use the magic words, "Tell me more." Because this is a FamilyMind response, the wife feels cared about, too.

A working couple with two children shared a similar problem. Both parents came home exhausted from work, and the kids were starved for both dinner and their parents' attention. By asking what their family needed at this crucial but chaotic time, these parents found a wonderful solution. Because everyone was hungry, tired, and wanted attention, they all sat down together in a favorite spot—the cool backyard or the comfortable family room—with snacks they prepared ahead of time. They used this time together to relax, to listen to each other's days, and to curb their gnawing hunger until dinner was ready. Sometimes the snacks are elaborate and nutritious enough to serve as the children's dinner, allowing the couple to reconnect by sharing an intimate dinner alone later.

The human heart can go to the lengths of God.

Dark and cold we may be, but this

Is no winter now. The frozen misery

Of centuries breaks, cracks, begins to move;

The thunder is the thunder of the floes,

The thaw, the flood, the upstart Spring.

Thank God our time is now when wrong

Comes up to face us everywhere,

Never to leave us till we take

The longest stride of soul men ever took.

Affairs are now soul size.

The enterprise

Is exploration into God.

Where are you making for? It takes

So many thousand years to wake,

But will you wake for pity's sake?[8]

—Christopher Fry, *A Sleep of Prisoners*

Endnotes: Part Six

1. Robert Johnson, *We: Understanding the Psychology of Romantic Love* (San Francisco: Harper and Row, 1983), 31.

2. Ibid., 30.

3. Deborah Tannen, *You Just Don't Understand* (New York: William Morrow and Company, 1990).

4. Maggie Scarf, *Intimate Worlds: Life Inside the Family* (New York: Random House, 1995), 36.

5. Coleman Barks and John Moyne, editors, *Open Secret* (Putney, VT: Threshold Books, 1984).

6. Angeles Arrien, *Gathering Medicine: Stories, Songs, and Methods for Soul-Retrieval*, audiocassette produced by Sounds True Recordings, Boulder, CO, 1994, Part One.

7. Angeles Arrien, *The Four-Fold Way* (San Francisco: Harper San Francisco, 1993).

8. Christopher Fry, *A Sleep of Prisoners* (London: Oxford University Press, 1951).

PART SEVEN

Houses and Other Obstacles to FamilyMind

Gammy used to say, "Too much scrubbing
takes the life right out of things..."
—Betty MacDonald, *The Egg and I*

S o far we know that making a family work takes a particular way of thinking we call FamilyMind. To think in FamilyMind we ask the question, "What does this family need now, including me?" It is as simple as that, right? Well, we also now know there are *obstacles* that get in the way of our thinking in FamilyMind—personal obstacles, such as old habits of behavior that land us in that hole in the sidewalk, a distrust or ignorance of our feelings, being on the overgiving or overreceiving side of give'ntake, and ignoring our likes and dislikes. We know that the core of family life, the family soul, needs constant nurturing to keep each member alive and thriving. The real purpose of family is to build relationships that support who we truly are. The obstacles that hinder building relationships are not only psychological. Other forces we live with every day move us toward isolation without our realizing it.

There are many obstacles outside of us that get in the way of living what Jungian therapist and master storyteller Clarissa Pinkola Estés, Ph.D., calls "the handmade life," the life made each day by our own hands.[1] Most of us lead such busy lives, we go on "automatic pilot" to get through the day without imagining we have any other choices. They are so ingrained into our world view that we no longer notice them. The obstacles that block our knowing what we really *really* need range from the individual to the global. Not only must we grapple with our personal, psychological issues, but we are also heavily influenced by the greater culture we live in.

Obstacle #One: The Fifties Ideal

How To Be A Good Housewife

Have dinner ready: Plan ahead, even the night before, to have a delicious meal on time. This is a way of letting him know that you have been thinking about and are concerned with his needs. Most men are hungry when they come home and the prospect of a good meal is part of the warm welcome needed.

Prepare yourself: Take fifteen minutes to rest so that you will be refreshed when he arrives. Touch up your make-up, put a ribbon in your hair and be fresh looking. He has just been with a lot of work-weary people. Be a little gay and a little more interesting. His boring day may need a lift.

Clean away the clutter: Make one last trip through the main part of the house just before your husband arrives, gathering up school books, toys, paper, etc. Then run a dust cloth over the tables. Your husband will feel he has reached a heaven of rest and order, and it will give you a lift too.

Prepare the children: Take a few minutes to wash the children's hands and faces (if they are small), comb their hair, and if necessary, change their clothes. They are little treasures and he would like to see them playing the part.

Minimize all noise: At the time of his arrival, eliminate all noise of the washer, dryer, dishwasher, or vacuum. Try to encourage the children to be quiet. Be happy to see him. Greet him with a warm smile and be glad to see him.

Some don'ts: Don't greet him with problems or complaints. Don't complain if he is late for dinner. Count this as minor compared to what he might have gone through that day. Make him comfortable. Have him lean back in a comfortable chair or suggest that he lie down in the bedroom. Have a cool or warm drink ready for him. Arrange his pillow and offer to take his shoes. Speak in a low, soft, soothing voice. Allow him to relax and unwind.

Listen to him: You may have a dozen things to tell him, but the moment of his arrival is not the time. Let him talk first.

Make the evening his: Never complain if he does not take you out to dinner or to other pleasant entertainment. Instead, try to understand his world of strain and pressure, his need to unwind and relax.

The goal: Try to make your home a place of peace and order where your husband can relax in body and spirit.[2]

Our seminar audiences respond with shocked disbelief, gleeful approval, silent anger, and nervous laughter to the above excerpt. Despite the fact that most of us today live in the difficult, uncharted territories of dual-income families, step-families, or single-parent families, we still use the 1950's, house-in-the-suburbs, two-parent, stay-at-home mom model of family life as the ideal. If only it were that simple. Unfortunately, the period of years we remember fondly as "the fifties" was an anomaly in our history, a time whose growth and abundance we are fairly unlikely to see again.[3] To continue to compare our lifestyle to an aberration is to keep ourselves stuck in the past and lost about how to live with our current challenges. As author Michael Elliott writes in his thought-provoking book, *The Day Before Yesterday*, Americans have become a country of whiners.[4] We don't want the limited roles of the fifties, but we look back to that time with nostalgia, wishing everything here would get back to "normal."

> *In our neighborhood, if the yard goes unmowed for a few days, you get looks from the neighbors like, "Well, when are you going to clean up the place?" I struggle every day to keep the inside as clean as my mother kept her house. With three kids, a part-time job, volunteer work at school, cooking, and shopping, I'm always*

*exhausted. I don't remember the last time my husband
and I sat down and really talked. I keep wondering, when
will my real life start?*

—*Shirley, forty-nine*

Author and educator Angeles Arrien, Ph.D., teaches us not to normalize the abnormal.[5] By normalizing an abnormal time in our past, we continue to yearn for something that was never really real and does not fit our present conditions. We believed that Ozzie and Harriet always knew what to do in any parenting situation, and that Donna Reed always looked beautiful while doing housework. If we could just sing like *The Partridge Family*, and get along like *The Brady Bunch*, we would lead perfect lives. We reject solutions to our current family problems, while complaining that it's not the "good ole days."

Solution #One

First ask, "What does this family need now, including me?" Our times call for unusual solutions to difficult problems, because we are in a major cultural transition. The rules of the past no longer apply. As long as we continue to compare ourselves to a forty-plus-year-old ideal—a past that existed for an extremely short period of time—we will stay stuck in an attitude of failure, of never measuring up, of being second-best. Our only dependable guide in these times is knowing what we really, really need.

Many mothers no longer have the luxury to stay home when their children are young. We desperately need caring, convenient, and affordable daycare. Many of today's families are headed by single parents. We must have supportive communities that provide affordable housing, efficient transportation services, and programs that benefit parents and families. We are all overburdened and stressed out from trying to maintain a lifestyle that takes us farther and farther away from our spiritual selves. We each require time and space for silence, for meditation, or to be outdoors, the opportunity to express ourselves through painting, singing, or dancing, and the freedom to laugh and dream. These are not luxuries—these are essentials for the human soul.

It is within the family that we find the solutions to the problems of today. By talking together and asking, "What do we *really*, **really** need?" we address current issues and realistically approach our lives. We must ask, "What does this family really, really need to keep our kids off drugs?" "What do we really, really need to get out of debt?" "What do we really, really need to care for Grandma?" "What do we really, really need to make our local high school safer?" "What do we really, really need to face Mom's alcoholism?"

Throwing out the fifties ideal as a measuring stick leaves us free to design a new standard. Our comparisons might look like this:

The Fifties Ideal

- Must have 2 cars.

- Must have big house in the hills.

- Must have 2 kids.

- Must mow lawn twice weekly.

- Junior must play baseball, basketball, and swim.

- Everyone has a TV in every room.

- Dad works outside the home. Mom works inside the home.

- Dad works hard to give family a sufficient income.

- Women and girls are good cooks, homemakers, and hostesses. They are quiet, cheerful, obedient, and loving.

- Men and boys are tough, strong, unemotional, and confident. They work hard to meet company goals.

- Good girls don't, and real boys score.

What is Ideal for Our Family?

- Do we really need 2 cars?

- Where do we really want to live?

- Do we really want a family?

- What do we really want to grow in our yard?

- What does Junior really need and want to do?

- Does TV really fit in our lifestyle?

- What does our family really need from Mom and Dad? What do they need to do?

- How much money does this family really need to be happy?

- Do women and girls have what they need to be who they truly are?

- What do men and boys really need to become to be who they truly are?

- What do our kids really need to be able to develop a healthy sexuality?

These comparisons could go on and on, and they do every day in our minds. The point is, we need standards that work for *our* times, a standard that is directed inward, rather than directed outward. Asking, "Does my family look as good as the Jones'," never proved anything. Asking, "How do my family members feel about themselves, each other, and the family group? Does our family work? Are we developing in ways that are satisfying to individual members and strengthening to the family? Are we contributing to a larger community? Are we helping to make the earth a better place to live?" encourages the kind of soul-searching required of us today as we meet the challenges of the coming century.

Obstacle #Two: The One-Butt Kitchen

We find other expectations and attitudes from the "good ole days" woven throughout many of the obstacles to thinking in FamilyMind. After World War II, the weapons industry shifted its perspective from making guns to making life easier for the housewife in the production of home gadgets and appliances. Each product reduced the number of people required to do household chores, and the "one-butt kitchen" was invented. Architecture became an obstacle to family interaction. Meal preparation was no longer a family affair, because the new kitchen was designed for the housewife to stand in one place and push buttons that sliced the food, diced the food, and cooked the food. The kitchen "breakfast bar" became popular, because it was designed for quick meals and easy clean-up. Family members sat alone or side-by-side, lined up in a row on stools facing front. The time family members spent in the kitchen in storytelling, laughing, and working together went the way of the wringer washer and the dodo—obsolete and extinct.

Another war relic still with us today is the attitude that housework is considered "shitwork," instead of being seen as creating a beautiful space where our families can live and thrive. In the designs of the post-war government and industry, shitwork—the endless chores we do in and outside the home—had to be eliminated to allow more leisure time, a better life, and the pursuit of individual happiness. We apologize if its use here is offensive, but we knew everyone would know what we mean, and how better to describe those tasks that must be done, but that no one values? Therefore, please pardon our colloquialism!

To boost the economy and secure happiness for all, the war on shitwork was declared. The target was the American home. Victory depended upon how many push-button gadgets industry could make and the consumer would buy. Munitions factories were converted to appliance factories, and sales soared so high that new plants had to be built. Automatic washers, dryers, refrigerators, dish washers, vacuum cleaners, timed ovens, ice, soda, and food dispensers, car washes, and automatic car transmissions became the rage; even an automatic lawn mower, guaranteed to cut the grass while you lie in the shade, sipping iced tea. Everyone rushed to buy the newest model promising to make life easier, cleaner, and freer. We learned to think, "Household chores are drudgery. We must do them as quickly as possible, so we can have fun." What the family used to think of as things that must be done to make a house a home were now regarded as yucky, distasteful shitwork.

I'll always remember my granny's dining room table. She polished it every week with her own special formula that smelled of lavender, until it shone like dark glass.

She took special pride in that table, and I also remember how candlelight reflected off its surface at family dinners. It radiated a peace and well-being I have been unable to recapture in my own family. I had a sense that we were all there safely together, protected from the changing world outside. If I have a chance to dust at all, my dining table gets two swipes. Forget the polish—I don't have time for it.

—Crystal, twenty-nine

Who Won?

Although the push-button industry was victorious in getting automation in every home, this is a war where we wonder who the winners are. When we stop to examine our lives, do we *really* have more leisure time to pursue happiness? Is life easier? Are we happier now that we can do the shitwork with the touch of a button? In some ways, automation has actually complicated our lives, because most of the tasks now have to be done by adults in isolation. Consider the dishwasher, for example. Most dishwashers have to be loaded in a certain way, and until children are older, the task is beyond them. Vacuuming is another chore that an adult or older child does alone. Family members scatter because of the noise, and no one is needed to hold the dustpan. Before the war on shitwork was declared, family members connected around the little things out of necessity, but push-button technology has brought division and separation, rather than more happiness and leisure. The big and little tasks were transformed into shitwork, and family togetherness became a casualty.

Solution #Two

Ask the question, "What does this family need now, including me?" We do not advocate a return to the past, but using the manual tasks of the household—*the little things*—to gather family members together creates more leisure time *and* builds family relationships. Household chores provide a structure and set the rhythm of the day.

When a family decides together what really, really needs to be done, the tasks take on new meaning. Of course, there will be complaints, arguments, and resistance—the FamilyMind Question does not make life perfect, but everyone will have to work it out to get it done. Family members will get to know each other. Children, especially ages eight through twelve, cooperate more readily when they see a purpose for their efforts or know they can perform a task that no one else can.

> *While I fix breakfast before school, Elizabeth knows that she's the only one available and capable of helping little Rosie get dressed. She does this task with an air of cheerful authority. If I ask her to fold laundry, she'd sniff and say, "Fold laundry? You can do that, Mom!"*
>
> *—Laura, mother of three*

The kitchens of the past were often the sites of family storytelling. Family history, folk wisdom, and good advice were shared by adults with the children as bread was baked, meals were prepared, and dishes were washed. To build a larger kitchen with room for a whole family to work in will not be an option for most of us. We can find places, however, to pass on our family lore. While we fold laundry, we can tell about when Granny was stranded in a flood; or how Granddad worked as a cattle inspector on the Kansas plains; of how Aunt Jessie rode a pig around the fair; and that Uncle Henry survived a fall off the barn roof into the horse trough. Or about the time Dad went to Burger King, paid the money at the drive-through window, and came home without the food; and the time when Mom put the birthday cake on top of the car to open the car door, got in forgetting it was there, drove clear across town with people honking and pointing at her, pulled into the driveway at home, and the cake was still there! Pulling weeds or harvesting the cherry tomato crop provides an opportunity for a mother to tell her daughter about her first period, her first kiss, her first prom. We love the story about the Easter ham. A daughter asked her mother why she cut the end off the Easter ham. The mother replied, "My mother taught me to do it." "But, why," asked the daughter, "Did Grandma cut it off?" "I don't know. Let's call her and ask," suggested the mother. Grandma said, "Oh, my mother always did that. I don't know why." Then great-aunt Maude lets them all know that her sister cut the end off the Easter ham, because her pan was too small!

> *I'm a single mom, and the time after school until bedtime was always the point in the day that I'd lose it. Some days I'd want to go to my bedroom, slam the door, and let the kids fend for themselves. The typical scenario started with me in the kitchen getting dinner with the boys in their bedrooms doing their homework. This never lasted, of course. I'd soon hear the boys fighting over what TV program to watch, and I'd storm back there with murder on my mind. I have great memories of my brother and me doing our homework at the kitchen table, while Mom cooked, but our apartment kitchen is too small, and the boys' desks are in their bedrooms. Finally, I decided that being a little crowded was better than the fighting, so I set up a card table in the kitchen doorway for the boys to do their homework on. This worked fine for about a week. Then they were taking a break every fifteen minutes to see what I was cooking, to sample, and to take part. This was even better. The boys got their homework done, and we eventually got dinner on. Now they help me plan meals, shop, and even take charge of the cooking, occasionally. The key is to keep everything as simple as possible.*
>
> *—Janice, forty-three*

Another part of the solution to the one-butt kitchen is to carefully decide whether or not the family really needs a certain machine or appliance. Dishwashers are an asset, for example, because they do save time and water. But, do we really need that bread machine, pasta maker, blender, electric knife, and so on? We may decide that we do, but the important thing to ask before adding more gadgets to the household inventory is, "Do we really, really need this? Will it help us function more efficiently and bring us together, or will it drive us apart?" Of course, there will be instances when we must forfeit togetherness to save time, but allowing our machines to interfere with family connections turns housework into shitwork, rather than *shared*work.

Obstacle #Three: Sex-Role Stereotypes and Cultural Expectations

In premodern tribal groups an individual's role was assigned according to gender and an inherited talent or position. Men hunted; women prepared the food. The role of chief passed from father to son, and the tribe looked for a new flint-maker among the old flint-maker's offspring. Choices were limited, but each role held honor and respect, because of its value to the survival of the tribe. These traditionally prescribed roles altered very little, often lasting for many generations.

Changes in the natural environment, such as the climate and game supply, mandated changes in early human society. New living conditions required a shift in roles to accommodate the shift in needs. Our history relives the tortoise and the hare story over and over again. The hare—environmental change—leaps forward, leaving the tortoise—social roles based on needs—behind in the dust. When social roles are no longer directly related to a society's survival, its members feel meaningless and question the *status quo*. The needs have changed, but the role requirements have not. Until the tortoise catches up, traditions are broken, revolt occurs, a new order breaks through, and appropriate roles that once again meet the survival needs of the society are adopted. This is where the family is headed today. Roles do not reflect the current needs of the family, leaving parents and children unsure of their place and purpose.

World War II ushered in a new race between the tortoise and the hare. Roles were loosened as the war effort demanded that women fill jobs created by the weapons industry, as well as the vacant job slots men left behind. The industrial-economic complex took on greater and greater power as it expanded to meet the needs of a war-based economy. The war's end brought about another shift in both social and economic needs. As families were reunited, home and all it stood for became the focus of life. The Husband bought the house and went to work to pay for it. The Wife took care of the house, making it a cozy castle for her man to come home to. Deviation from these roles usually meant trouble.

Today, everything is out of whack! Many of us grew up with sex-role stereotypes firmly entrenched with the fifties ideal. Some of us had mothers devoted to the women's movement of the late sixties and early seventies, who fought for the opportunity to choose their own roles. The clash of these two, strongly-held positions within the same family is a clash of titans!

When a woman and a man make a home together, there are so many big and little things to be worked out between them. This may go smoothly at first, but difficulties usually arise around the household tasks.

Woman + Man + Household chores = TENSION

If the couple have good communication, a satisfying sexual relationship, and are relatively happy in their jobs, then household chores are merely an irritant. A good friend of ours says, "I go easy on my husband, because I know he just didn't learn how to take care of a house when he was little, so I end up being the one to notice things that need to be done. We agreed that he will follow a list I make for him. I have to go slowly, have patience, and explain with a great deal of tact how some things are done."

After children arrive, the big and little things become more important, even crucial to the happiness and survival of the family. Certain oversights or neglect might mean the difference between safety and injury to a baby. The household chores and the thinking required become magnified a thousand times.

Woman + Man + *Children* + Household chores = BOOM

Cynthia and I got along pretty well during our first two years of marriage. Of course, there was the usual working out of how well the kitchen was cleaned, squeezing the toothpaste in the middle of the tube, and my picking up my clothes from the floor of the closet, but the little things didn't seem to bother us too much. After our first kid was born, the bottom fell out. No matter what I did to help, it was never enough, or never good enough. I became super critical of how she did things, too. The house was never clean enough for me; dinner was never on time; the kid's toys were always underfoot. Every room was a battleground over little stuff that really shouldn't mean very much.

—Jon, thirty

Another familiar scenario involves the wife and mother of a family as the sole keeper of the home and family life.

As I furiously stuff dirty clothes into the washing machine, I think, "I've asked Helen a dozen times to do this laundry, and it's still not done! Jeremy's knights are all over the living room, and Howard is out puttering in his workshop. I feel like the maid, who never gets a day off, help, or appreciation around here. How can I keep this house clean all by myself?"

—Julie, thirty-eight

The mother doing laundry spends most of her time at home picking up and cleaning. She feels like a troop commander, ordering her family to pick up this, put away that. Her ten-year-old son says, "Mom, every time I see you, you greet me by telling me to do something, like pick up my toys or put my books away. That's all you ever talk about!" Helen, age fourteen, hides out in her room with earphones blaring, hoping her mother won't find her. Their father Howard, sneaks around the house, trying to avoid his wife's criticism and complaints. Whenever the wife tries to talk to him about her frustrations, their communication usually ends like this:

THE Argument

She says: You never do *anything* around the house!

He says: What do you mean? I do the dishes; I pick up the kids; I mow the lawn!!!!

She says: There you go again, wanting medals and applause for helping out.

He says: I don't want medals! I'm just responding to your accusations about my not doing anything around the house.

She says: (Sigh) This isn't about *things*.

He says: (Looking a bit wild-eyed) If it isn't about *things*, why did you say I don't do *anything* around the house?

She says: You never listen to me. You're never *here*.

He says: What do you mean, never here??? I took off an extra day's work for a three-day weekend. I've been working on all these projects that have been sitting around because of how busy we are... (He looks up in the middle of his sentence, and she is gone.)

She walks away feeling angry, hurt, and hopeless. He walks away feeling crazy and confused, his brain working overtime to figure out this mysterious *thing* he isn't doing. If he wasn't here all weekend, where did she think he was? [6]

What gets us into THE Argument? Making assumptions and acting as though they are true is probably the most common cause. Most of us enter relationships assuming that we and our mate will fill certain roles. These role expectations are based on a number of influences. Family customs become ingrained within us from childhood, and we mistakenly believe that other families are just like our own. Our social class experiences determine our social values. Our level of

education affects our goals and ambitions in life. The gender training, both conscious and unconscious, that we receive as children sets
us rigidly or flexibly in relationship with others. Based on these
early lessons, we make assumptions about our mates that are not
necessarily true for them. If we come from a family of doctors or
lawyers, we might assume that our mates be ambitiously engaged in
the helping professions. If we learned that girls are overly emotional
and that real boys don't cry, then we may assume that crying shows
weakness and be unable to tolerate it in our significant others. If we
were taught that men do one thing and women do another, such
rigid role assignments often lead into THE Argument, because the
needs of our families may not be reflected in the roles each partner
assumes.

THE Argument is not really about *things*. It is about making sure
that group needs are considered and acted upon. The *she* in THE
Argument feels angry, because she feels trapped into doing the thinking
for the family, and has to hand out assignments. The *he* is doing what
he has been told, but feels criticized for it. He does not realize that his
not helping to make the list is part of the problem. He is doing his best
to get everything done, but he is out of touch with the needs of the
family. The woman might say, "Oh sure, my husband does things
around the house—when dinner is ready, he decides to take the videos
back to the store, while we wait dinner on him!" The man feels
confused and crazy, because although he is completing the things on
the list, he has not learned to orchestrate his *doing* according to what is
needed by everyone else in the family. The assumption that one spouse
does the thinking *and* the doing while the other spouse does the doing
rather poorly, leaves each at odds with the other.

Without knowing how to resolve our conflicts together, we get
caught in THE Argument with cycles of anger, resentment, attack,
withdrawal, failure, and blame. We begin to feel taken advantage of,
separate, and isolated from each other. Our emotional connection
breaks, and we begin to lead parallel lives. We eventually resign ourselves to the situation, dream of being alone, question our choice of
mate, or consider a divorce. We have reached a psychological separation. Many couples seek counseling at this point. Others choose

physical separation, often ending in divorce, and then face it all over again with someone else. Some of us struggle along trying to find connection and happiness through our children, other relationships, affairs, or our careers.

It is easy to get stuck in certain roles before we even realize it, often because our mothers or fathers did them, or because of cultural expectations.

> **JEANNE** | My father always drove the car, so I always expected my husband to drive. My mother did the ironing, so I thought I should do it in my own home. In reality, I feel safer when I drive, and Don has many more clothes that require ironing, so he does the ironing in our family. I love it!

Solution #Three

"What does this family need now, including me?" Assigning or accepting roles that fit what our family group needs and learning to do them in a meaningful way may bring a few surprises. If Mom loves weeding the garden or mowing the lawn, these tasks will be far less tedious for her than if Dad grudgingly does them because his father did. We may find that our children are more cooperative and involved with family chores when their completion makes it possible for a beloved family activity, such as singing, storytelling, or playing games. Couples may find sparks rekindled between them, because they are breaking old habits of protecting and isolating themselves. They no longer get lost in the resentment of being in a role, "just because." Asking, "What does this family need now, including me?" brings us into the present and out of blame, anger, and resentment. We may wonder what all the fireworks were about, because Family-Mind thinking allows us to hear grievances, desires, and needs. Negotiation, compromise, and resolution naturally follow.

My wife constantly complained that she does most of the work, and I contribute when it's convenient. We argued

most of the time. After we learned about FamilyMind,
we were able to talk about what things our family needs
with less anger, but it was still tense between us. One
evening I came home from work spent, and as I walked
in I thought, "I can't take this FamilyMind garbage
tonight. I need some time to myself!" I plopped down on
the couch without saying anything to anyone. After a
few minutes, I heard my wife's footsteps and thought,
"Here it comes; she's going to let me have it for not
helping out while she's had a hard day, too." She sat
down next to me and handed me a plate of snacks and
said, "Here, Honey. You look like you've had a hard day.
Since we're all so tired, let's go out to eat after you've
rested a bit." I was shocked. I got what I had been
wanting all our married life: affection and care. Then it
dawned on me. "If I think of others first, along with my
own needs, they will also think of me first." What a con-
cept. I felt stupid for not seeing it, but I guess you have
to live it to get it!

—Mike, thirty-two

Every couple has their own version of THE Argument. It may follow
more along the lines of, "You didn't clean up after your snack," or
"You always leave the lights on all over the house." But, the essence
is usually the same: Both people feel overwhelmed, alone, and needy.
We do not mean to imply that couples should never have THE
Argument, or that if we always use FamilyMind, we will always avoid
THE Argument. Hopefully, THE Argument will become a signal to
ask some form of the FamilyMind Question, "What do we need
right now?" Or, "What is this argument really about? What needs
are not being met?" "Am I stuck in a role that I hate, don't know
about, don't do well, or is burdensome to me?"

Families bound by traditional roles do what they assume is right by
following an external set of rules, whether or not they meet the actual
needs of the family. Such role-bound families may wonder why they

enter therapy on the brink of divorce. In their couple's work together they discover that societal roles, rules, and beliefs must be personalized to fit individual family needs. Role-flexible families, on the other hand, are those that fill roles and complete tasks based on the needs of everyone in the family. They will be better able to face the many changes and challenges of daily life.

Many of us struggling today to raise young children, pursue a career, and keep up a home often feel a sense of isolation, of loneliness, of going against the grain, of swimming through molasses. No matter how hard we work, we seem to be getting nowhere. We waver back and forth between roles. Many parents, especially the fathers we talk with, say with regret that they feel they do not really belong in their family groups.

> *Sure, I come home every night, and my kids love me, but somehow I don't really fit. You know? My wife and I make all the big decisions together, and we agree on most stuff, but it seems she still runs the home. We all look to her for the little important things about home. She complains that I'm somehow just not there, but I don't know how to change that. I don't know what she wants me to do.*
>
> —*Jon, twenty-nine, father of two*

Imagine returning home after a long day at work. Pause outside the front door, and take a deep breath. We form the question in our minds, "What does this family need?" Panic buttons may go off; we may feel a momentary surge of anger. We are only human, after all, and have had a long, exhausting day at work. We then remember that the question, "What does this family need?" includes *us*, because we are part of this family group. *FamilyMind thinking includes everybody.* We also remember that asking, "What does this family need, including me?" does *not* mean that we, alone, must be responsible for taking care of everyone's needs. We take another deep breath and enter our home, knowing that our needs can be considered with all the rest. We, too, belong to this family group.

Obstacle #Four:
So Many Needs, So Little Time

To create a healthy family, individual members must have as many needs met as possible. Of course, we can not *all* have *all* we want and need *all* of the time. There simply is not enough money, time, and energy to go around, as much as we would like to create it. The pressing and never-ending needs of children, especially when they are young, can seem overwhelming to parents, and we mistakenly assume we must put all our own needs aside, becoming more and more burned out, resentful, and frustrated. The fact is we *do* have to postpone or delay gratification of our desires at various points during our parenting lives. Perhaps the kids are too young to take that coveted Caribbean cruise; we may need to put off the longed-for career change until our children are in school; maybe we would love to quit our job and be a full-time mom, but our daughter's need for corrective surgery makes that extra income necessary now.

The little, everyday needs—the ones that do not seem so important and so get shuffled to the end of the list—are the ones that require the consideration of FamilyMind. Having time for quiet solitude to ponder the important questions of our lives, time for the inner work necessary for spiritual growth, time for fun, time to daydream or watch the clouds, enough time to rest to be able to respond with love to the unlimited demands of our children—all are vital for creating healthy homes. However, the truth of the matter is that especially when our children are small, there is rarely time for quiet moments alone. Maybe, if we have a lock on the bathroom door, we get fifteen minutes for a bubble bath, but some days we are lucky to even get a quick shower! When both parents work outside the home, life becomes even more hectic, as we do laundry, plan meals, shop, cook, and spend time with our children between the cracks of career demands. How do we find time to be whole human beings?

Solution #Four

Our search for the answer to this important question usually leads us to seek time apart, alone, *away* from the family. The solution, however, lies *within* the family and the practice of FamilyMind. Lay minister Ernest Boyer, Jr. writes in his remarkable book, *A Way in the World: Family Life as Spiritual Discipline*, that family life provides an opportunity to live, what he calls, the sacrament of care. Choosing to live in a family with group mindfulness benefits those receiving the care as well as those giving it.

It is a difficult life, difficult in the attentiveness and energy it asks. Care is constant. It is likely to be most needed at exactly those times you yourself feel least able to give it. It is difficult, too, because it asks you to see the extent of your own limitations.

But this life can be difficult for an entirely different reason. All of these never-ending, everyday tasks can seem far from what is most important in life and that probably more than anything else makes them hard to endure. It is not easy to see how each of these acts, so fleeting in itself, adds up to much more collectively. How hard it is to give yourself to something that seems to have so little significance!

...To live this life is to participate in the mystery of the divine and to become a partner in that ongoing act of creation, the forming of the love from which all else is formed.[7]

—Ernest Boyer, Jr., *A Way in the World*

Don For much of my married life, I tried to escape the endlessness of dinner dishes, bills, late night baby struggles, the never-quite-done-ironing, and the mysterious arguments about it all, by fantasizing about long trips alone. The more intense the demands of home, the more I wanted a football game to take me away.

My longing to escape the needs of home has lessened after learning to use FamilyMind thinking. I used to look for what *things* needed to be done. Concentrating on *things* tended to take me out of the family group and make me wish I were someplace else, doing something worthwhile, making me feel appreciated. Now, when I ask, "What are our needs right now, and how can we meet them together?" I move from my frustrated head-thinking into the heart of family need. Checking out what the group needs—remembering that the group includes me—changes my lists of *things* into activities that connect us as a family, ways of giving and receiving that have purpose and meaning. When I enter into activities with a focus on immediate, genuine needs and wants, I feel a wonderful sense of belonging. Rather than feeling like a robot doing *things*, I am part of a creative act, an act of care that feeds my soul, nurtures my family, *and* gets things done.

Surprisingly, my efforts toward meeting real family needs make me feel refreshed and satisfied. In the past, when I hurried through a list of chores, I felt unappreciated and exhausted. Each task felt like a five-hundred-pound weight, and I resented my family's demands. Listening for genuine needs, especially when they are different from what I want, are now a delightful challenge and focus me in the here and how.

FamilyMind has taught me that a list of chores is not important for its own sake. I no longer resentfully jump in to do them, because they are there, and it is my job to do them. Knowing that *things* are important only in relationship to people, I now ask, "Does this task meet a real need here?" This question helps me to prioritize tasks based on care, rather than on the accomplishment of goals that "should" be done.

The most amazing thing to me about it all is that my own needs for closeness, for belonging, and for sharing are usually met. The more I listen, ask, and act with care, the more my family responds to my real needs and wants. They encourage me to nap, take it easier, and take a break. I feel appreciated for what I do. My focus on others in a way that includes myself makes me feel more alive, emotionally open, and able to ask for help. I can more easily accept feedback when I make mistakes and forget things, too. It's funny. Now my family says, "Go to the 'Forty-niner' game. You'll love it." Before, I would have felt guilty about going on a weekend and resentful that everybody wants *from* me but no one gives *to* me. Now, when my friend Bob calls at the last minute with that extra ticket, I hesitate, but not because of guilt and resentment. Now, I actually hesitate because, if I go, I will miss my day at home. Don't misunderstand me. I *do* hesitate, but then I quickly run to the car and hope I make it by kickoff time.

The problem is not the *things* a man wants and needs for himself in a family; it is the way he *thinks* about the things he wishes for. Most men want to feel they belong in their families, but don't know how or can't figure out what they need to do differently. The real question is not, "What can I *do* differently?" but, "How can I *think about* the big and little things in a richer, more meaningful way, for myself and us all?" As I answer that question, I begin to learn what comes from genuine giving and receiving with people I love. Now I *know* I am really home. A man feels he can actually fly when he is lifted by the magic of belonging to a group called "his family."

Obstacle #Five:
The Homogenization of America

Automation ushered in a new era in the race between the tortoise and the hare. The appliance with the most influence upon social roles was the television set. Never before could so many people be mesmerized and swayed to buy so many products so quickly. We bought goods that promised to bring us happiness, whether or not we really needed or wanted them. We bought the American Dream, because the consumer-products industry not only sold things; it sold fantasies. The ads told us that there were riches and leisure to be had if we worked hard enough for them. We all could be beautiful, successful, rich, slender, desired, sophisticated, and happy if we just do what everyone else does and buy *this*! Television shaped the needs, wants, and wishes of the American public to meet the needs, wants, and wishes of a few advertising executives and businessmen. Today, how much we buy into the cultural expectations of consumerism defines who we are. Many of us find ourselves pursuing someone else's dreams and living someone else's life, because we are caught in the cultural trance of materialism. We believe we need *things* to be happy.

The degree to which we allow technology to regulate our activities influences the degree to which we participate in what is real. A truly dangerous aspect of television's hypnotic hold is that the lines between fantasy and real life become blurred. The distinction between truth and appearances become suspect. The difference between education and entertainment become unclear.

Our familial and social roles have also shifted to meet the times. The breakdown of a large Russian American immigrant family is beautifully and poignantly portrayed in the movie *Avalon*.[8] During the first half of the film, we meet several generations of this demonstrative, close-knit family who live packed together in an urban neighborhood in the 1930s. Their family dinners are loud, argumentative gatherings with serious discussions about how to raise enough money to bring relatives still living in Europe to America, while children climb in and out of laps, under and around a big table laden with a traditional meal. One member's success is everyone's success; one member's tragedy marks them all. Sons work alongside fathers; daughters consult mothers; cousins play with cousins; aunts gossip together; uncles scheme and argue; they laugh; they cry together.

In the second half of the film, television enters their lives, and the fabric that held them together begins to unravel, bit by precious bit. One branch of the family buys a house in the suburbs; grandchildren have no time for grandparents; in-laws become estranged; the family get-togethers are few and far between with most of the communicating done by telephone; and saddest of all, the family meals became silent affairs on TV trays in front of the television.

The social roles depicted on television created isolation, competition, and suspicion between the generations. The families in the film lost touch with their real needs. Their roles no longer related to the needs of the group. The men went to work and commuted long hours to earn enough money to provide the things their families thought they needed. The women were trapped in the endless routines of housework and child care. The children learned to want more, bigger, better, and newer. A different standard emerged for family life: Look good on the outside, feel empty on the inside. And many of us live with these values today.

Modern cultural forces inundate families via television with confusing and conflicting messages about boys and girls, women and men, minorities and the disadvantaged. In our grandparents' generation, cultural values and mores went unquestioned by most families, and children were fairly consistently taught the rules of social behavior, self-esteem, family responsibility, work ethics, and community commitment. Today, however, many of us feel we must protect our children from the influences of cultural stereotypes. Questions like the following drive us mad:

Should girls play with Barbies?

Should boys have toy guns?

Does television provoke violence in children?

Do computers affect learning?

When should girls start wearing makeup?

Why is my eight-year-old daughter on a diet?

How can I help my son enjoy school?

How many hours of TV should children watch per day?

Is it okay if my son doesn't like sports?

Is it okay if my daughter doesn't like sports?

How do I keep my kids off drugs?

When do I tell my daughter about menstruation?

When do I talk to my kids about sex?

The list is endless, and the consequences can be serious. An eight-year-old girl who is dieting, because her body is putting on fat—doing what comes naturally around eight, nine, or ten in preparation for the onset of menstruation—is headed for trouble. We must counteract the cultural stereotypes of a tall, thin, perfect body and help her accept nature's way for eight-year-olds. A boy having difficulty in second grade sets up a long rap sheet in his school files that advance with him from grade to grade, influencing teacher expectations that often determine his learning behavior and achievements.

Our children learn that they must be like everyone else, have what everyone else has, and do what everyone else does to be successful, to belong, and to be loved. Individual needs and differences become either lost or ridiculed: Fat people are lazy or silly. Blacks are sport stars or foolish. Hispanics are poor or gang members. Women are dumb or bossy. The disabled are invisible. Street people are dishonest or crazy.

Solution #Five

"What does this family need now, including me?" We wish we could snap ourselves out of this cultural trance by simply throwing out the television set. Our problems, however, are not with television *per se*; our problems come from *how* we use television. Television is great for discriminating adults who choose to watch for entertainment or education. However, we have allowed television to take control of our lives. To find solutions, we must know what TV does for us. For many it provides background noise while we go about daily chores. For others it provides company, something to fill empty, lonely hours. Some of us use it as a distraction from the day's hassles. We use it as a babysitter, mesmerizing the kids so we can have a few moments of peace. Program guides may dictate our routines, with social events scheduled around our favorite, not-to-be-missed shows. TV characters may become as real as our own friends and families, and we can live vicariously through them, rather than have to face the inconvenience or pain of actual family interactions or conflicts. For children, especially, television can become real life. How far will we go before we confuse watching a football game with playing one;

following a travel video with taking a trip; acting out our anger through TV murder and mayhem; and spending more time with a TV family than we do with our own?

For more insight into the role that television plays in our lives, we must ask ourselves the following questions:

How many hours per day do I, or my children, watch TV?

Does my family fight over anything having to do with TV?

Do I watch TV rather than doing something else, because it is easier?

Do I let my children watch TV, so that I can have some alone time?

How often do we watch TV during the day when we could be outdoors?

How often do we watch TV rather than doing something with other family members, such as take a walk, go for a drive, play cards, read aloud, bake some cookies, do a jigsaw puzzle, and so on?

Do we eat family meals in front of the TV?

Do I often describe plots from TV shows when I'm with family members or friends?

Would I rather watch a favorite show than do something with a family member or friend?

Are any of my children having difficulty learning to read, paying attention in school, or sitting still for reasonable periods of time, such as during church or at a family meal?

How am I affected by the violence I read or hear about on the news? The violence in my neighborhood? My child's school? My own home?

Is our social schedule arranged around the TV?

Does our placement of furniture invite conversation, or is it set up strictly for television viewing?

If the answers to these questions indicate that television is taking the place of real family life, then we may want to examine what we are trying to avoid and what we really, really need to re-create a more authentic life. We must ask ourselves:

Did I live today the way I truly wanted to?

Did I use every opportunity to listen to my children?

Did I communicate effectively with my mate?

Did I do something helpful for another person today?

Did I do something for myself that I truly love?

Did I learn something new about a family member today? About myself?

Am I living a life that I want my children to model?

How do I want to be remembered after I die?

Because television is the primary mode of spreading cultural values today, we urge parents to consider what life lessons our children are learning from TV. In ancient cultures, the teaching stories were carefully chosen to develop confidence, honesty, cooperation, and compassion in children. When it was time to take their places as adult members of the tribe, they took on their responsibilities with honor and integrity. What stories do our children hear and see? Who creates these stories? What moral lessons do they learn from "Beavis and Butthead?" "Aladdin?" "The Simpsons?" What values do our children need to be able to face the challenges they will meet in the year 2020?

The solution to the homogenization and mass marketing of our culture contains more questions than answers, because there is no single answer for everyone. We must each find our own solutions. The good news is that there is a guiding question, "What does this family really need right now, including me?"

Endnotes: Part Seven

1. Clarissa Pinkola Estés, *The Red Shoes*, audiocassette produced by Sounds True Recordings, Boulder, CO, 1992.

2. Excerpted from a 1950s American high school Home Economics textbook as read on the Ronn Owens Show, KGO-AM Radio, San Francisco, CA, 1995. We apologize for not having complete resource information for this quote. We would like very much to give proper credit, and if anyone knows its source, we would be grateful for their writing to our publisher, Celestial Arts, P.O. Box 7123, Berkeley, CA.

3. Michael Elliott, *The Day Before Yesterday* (New York: Simon and Schuster, 1996).

4. Ibid.

5. Angeles Arrien, *Gathering Medicine: Stories, Songs, and Methods for Soul-Retrieval*, audiocassette produced by Sounds True Recordings, Boulder, CO, 1994, Part One.

6. Jeanne Elium and Don Elium, *Raising a Daughter: Parents and the Awakening of a Healthy Woman* (Berkeley, CA: Celestial Arts, 1994), 85-86.

7. Ernest Boyer, Jr., *A Way in the World: Family Life as Spiritual Discipline* (San Francisco: Harper and Row, 1984).

8. *Avalon*, directed and written by Barry Levinson, 1990.

PART EIGHT

Chocolate and Other Obstacles to FamilyMind

It is fitting that speed should be our chemical superstar.
With the only certainty in our daily existence being
change, and a rate of change growing always faster in
a kind of technological leapfrog game, speed helps
people to think they are keeping up.[1]

—Gail Sheehy, *Speed Is of the Essence*

Author Gail Sheehy aptly describes modern life as trying to keep up in a "kind of technological leapfrog game." When we find ourselves on such a runaway roller coaster, it is no wonder we look for ways to speed us up, slow us down, wake us up, and put us to sleep. The use of substances to help us get though our days and nights keeps us removed from what is going on in each moment of our lives. Beloved singer Pearl Bailey once said, "Sometimes I would almost rather have people take away years of my life than take away a moment."[2] Indeed, it is the precious moments we long remember, ponder over, gain strength from, and learn from. When we resort to caffeine, marijuana, alcohol, cigarettes, sugar, and other addictive drugs, we numb ourselves from the pain, as well as the joy, in our lives. We lose touch with what we, ourselves, and what others we love really, really need.

Caffeine

For many of us, the day is punctuated by numerous hits of caffeine: from that first cup of coffee or tea with or instead of breakfast;

followed by a morning coffee break at work; a coca cola with lunch; an afternoon coffee break with some chocolate to take care of that low blood sugar around three to four o'clock; and, finally, a cup of cocoa before bed. Five cups of java at work may get us through the last of the inventory, but at home it renders us pretty useless as a family negotiator. Too much caffeine revs most of us up and makes us more goal-oriented and activity-focused, rather than need-focused. We tend to become hyper, irritable, pushy, more easily angered and frustrated, and out of touch with what is really going on around us. When overusing caffeine, some of us find it very difficult to be around small children, because of the patience, attention, and sensitivity they require. The extravagant intake of caffeine allows little sensitivity toward anyone, particularly ourselves.

> *Like most computer programmers, I use the industry's official drink—coffee—to help me meet impossible deadlines. In my office, we're all wired, and it makes an exciting environment, as we create miracles out of nothing! I have recently learned, however, that drinking coffee at home causes nightmares, especially on the weekends. Being a tornado at home just doesn't mix with four kids, but I didn't realize it until my husband pointed out that I really wasn't getting as much done as I thought I was, and how hyper, short, and irritated I was towards him and the kids. The first week I tried drinking decaf, I felt like a lump, but I was amazed at how fights were fewer, mornings were calmer, and I enjoyed being with my husband in a softer, more enjoyable way. With caffeine I was busier, but I don't think I accomplished much compared to the work I had to do to repair the damage to my family relationships.*
>
> *—Inez, thirty-nine*

Recommended reading:

America's Favorite Drug, by Bonnie Edwards, Odonian Press, Tucson, AZ, 1992.

Marijuana

Smoking grass envelops us in a pleasurable fog, making us numb to our pain and to the pain of others. While high on marijuana, we can remain aloof from negativity, complaints, and criticism; our perceptions are slightly out of focus allowing us to remain just slightly out of touch with family dynamics. Some become addicted to the carefree feelings marijuana offers and lose their desire to be truly connected or involved with anything other than the pleasures of smoking. Many pot users suffer from chronic, low-grade depression and an agitated rage when not high. Other family members may become wary, uncomfortable, or even fearful around the smoker, because of this unpredictable behavior. The marijuana user becomes an ineffective, noncontributing family member. Because the habit often causes undue financial stress on a family, the user may resort to sneaking and lying and suffer guilt, thus further reducing his or her feeling of family membership and belonging. Therapists observe that the use of marijuana by clients reduces the effectiveness of psychotherapy and family counseling. Because they cannot get close to their real feelings, effective behavior changes are blocked. A family member zoned-out on grass becomes a silent, pseudo family member disconnected from what she or he really, really needs.

I've smoked grass since I was thirteen. It helped me deaden the hurt and anger of those early years after my parents' divorce. Then the fogging grew into a habit that became my style of coping with any stress. When I hear people say that grass isn't addictive, I shudder. It may not be for everyone, but it is for someone like me. When my first son was born, I used grass to cope with the strain of fatigue and financial worries. Now I'm thirty-one, and I have quit the drug, but I have a lot of catching and growing up to do. My chronic use of marijuana froze me emotionally in adolescence. Not only did I miss my own teen and early adult years, but I've missed out on my kids' early years. I was there in body, but grass put my mind and feelings someplace else. The hardest part to acknowledge is how seductive the drug is in taking me out of the loop of emotional belonging and caring in my family.

—Clark, thirty-one

Networks:

Marijuana Anonymous World Service Office
(800) 766-6779

Alcohol

Alcohol is a depressant that reduces our active participation in our families and in our own lives. People abuse alcohol in different ways. There is the *maintenance drinker*, who is basically functional while numb. They do not look dangerous, but they do not participate in family life. The *seasonal drinker* drinks to deal with emotional pain, usually on holidays, when family traditions and beliefs cause anxiety, arguments, disappointed expectations, and broken promises. This can be especially difficult for children, who shut down emotionally to protect themselves from the traumatic events caused by drinking. The *angry drinker* controls the family by making anger a taboo feeling. Because they have to avoid anger and the vital messages that anger can give, the family loses touch with what is important and what is not. The *raging drinker* operates from a chronic, low-level depression and is a walking time bomb just waiting to explode. When anyone in the family abuses alcohol, the incidence of violent behavior increases, and the possibility of sexual and other forms of physical abuse rises. Commitments, agreements, and promises made at various stages of intoxication will be forgotten when the drinker is sober, and too many disappointments will greatly diminish the group's trust in him or her. FamilyMind thinking becomes skewed within an alcoholic's family. Other family members often try to anticipate the needs of the drinker, whose needs become disproportionate to everyone else's. Children have to become more adult-like to care for the more child-like adult drinker, and many adult children of alcoholics rightfully lay claim to a lost childhood.

I mostly remember my father asleep in his recliner, a newspaper open over his chest. By the time I got home from school he was a walking autotron from booze, and after dinner he landed in his chair, and that was that. He was like a monument in our home that we all played and lived around. My mother said a lot under her breath, but never to him until I was fifteen, when she suddenly moved us kids into an apartment and divorced him. I never learned how to relate to a man, because Dad was simply not involved in our family. I was attracted to my husband because he showed me so much care and interest while we were dating. But after our first year of marriage and the birth of our first child, it was like a ghost showed up in our house and took over my mind and body. I started avoiding his touch, interest, and his care. When my husband finally insisted, I agreed to couple's therapy. Now I know where the ghost came from. I learned to be around a man who was uninvolved or distracted by drink or projects, and I got nervous when my husband was so present with me. We don't drink, but my father's use of alcohol taught me a habit of avoidance that prevented me from being able to focus on myself and others in a genuine and straightforward way. Now that I've met the ghost, it's up to me to make the changes.

—Kiri, twenty-seven

When I was drinking, I only drank once a month on weekends, but I always got totally wasted, and it took a good week to bring my family back together. I denied being alcoholic, because I didn't drink every day, and I never missed a day of work because of the booze. Except for that one weekend a month, I was fine. When I backed out into the street into an oncoming truck, endangering my youngest daughter and myself, I had to admit something was wrong. We all went into family counseling, and I discovered to my real surprise that my three kids and my wife were terrified of me all month.

They never knew when I would go on that weekend binge, and they were always waiting for the bomb to drop. I'm in recovery now and am working to make it up to my family. I thought I was being a good father and husband with only the usual blemishes that most men have. Come to find out, my blemishes are major crevices the size of the Grand Canyon, and my family still does not feel safe to share their real feelings around me. What do I need? I don't really know yet. I do know that I need to get at the reason I was drinking. I also know that I want to earn the right to give and receive love from my wife and kids.

—Sam, forty-six

I spent so much of my childhood in between my mother and father trying to stop their drunken fights that I jump in between my husband and kids whenever they have a disagreement. I act more like a policewoman than a wife and mother. My interfering in their working things out has caused more trouble than it has helped. Now they save problems up, and the weekends are full of uproars. I was creating the exact kind of scenes I swore I would never be part of. Counseling is helping me be better able to differentiate between levels of anger, and allow others to work out their differences. I'm also learning to express my own, long-ago-buried anger.

—Alana, thirty-two

Networks:

Alcoholics Anonymous General Service Office
Grand Central Station
P.O. Box 459
New York, NY 10163
(212) 870-3400

Alanon-Alateen Information Service
(800) 344-2666

Recommended reading:

It Will Never Happen To Me, by Claudia Black, M.A.C., Denver, CO, 1982.

Twelve Steps and Twelve Traditions, published by Alcoholics Anonymous World Services, New York, 1981.

Living Sober, published by Alcoholics Anonymous World Services, New York, 1975.

Smoking

Smoking is a powerful addiction to nicotine that initially acts as an upper, like an amphetamine, then gives way to a depressive, sedative state.[3] This addiction numbs the power of our feeling messengers, leaving our experiences of joy, grief, anger, and panic deadened or greatly reduced. The habit of smoking allows us to stay out of touch with our strong feelings. Smoking is also socially isolating thanks to the recent proliferation of antismoking legislation. Designated smoking areas are quickly becoming the norm in the private sector as well.

The menacing effects of smoking on the family range from serious health risks to actual death of a smoking family member. Parents who smoke increase the susceptibility of their young children to such respiratory diseases as pneumonia and bronchitis through exposure to secondhand smoke.[4] Nonsmoking spouses of smokers experience a greater risk of contracting lung cancer, and nearly half a million Americans die each year from the complications of smoking.[5]

> *After twenty years of smoking, I'm trying to stop, and I'm overwhelmed with anger and sadness. Several times I've become such a mushball, that I started again just to get back in control. Now, I'm in counseling to help me deal with these strong feelings. I hadn't realized how*

much my smoking was affecting family members until I got angry the other day and overheard my youngest son say, "OK, time to light one up on the porch." That jolted me into realizing how observant my kids are and how easily it is to teach habits that I don't want to be teaching.

—Parker, thirty-seven

Networks:

American Lung Association
1740 Broadway
New York, NY 10019
(212) 315-8700

American Cancer Society
(212) 586-8700

Action on Smoking and Health (ASH)
2013 H Street, NW
Washington, DC 20006
(202) 659-4310

Recommended reading:

You Can Stop Smoking, by Jacquelyn Rogers, Simon and Schuster, New York, 1977.

The No-Nag, No-Guilt, Do-It-Your-Own-Way Guide to Quitting Smoking, by Tom Ferguson, M.D., Ballantine Books, New York, 1987.

How To Quit Smoking Without Gaining Weight, by Martin Katahn, Norton, New York, 1994.

Cigarette Confidential, by John Fahs, Berkeley Books, New York, 1996.

Sugar

Like coffee, sweets and desserts are stimulants that give us a temporary lift in energy. Chocolate also contains phenylethylamine, the same chemical released in our brain when we fall in love.[6] Chocolate and other sweets do seem to envelope most of us in feelings of well-being, but we get into trouble in several ways when we use them too often. Sweets usually contain large amounts of fat and sugar and can cause difficulties in maintaining the appropriate body weight when consumed excessively. If these "comfort foods" are used to replace personal affection and closeness, we become distant and detached from our feelings. We may notice dramatic mood swings and unpredictable behavior in ourselves or others who are sugar-dependent. People with a history of sexual or physical abuse tend to overuse sugar. The feelings of well-being from eating sugar and chocolate help to keep us outwardly focused and unaware of our inner pain.

> *Growing up in my family was almost like growing up with an alcoholic. My mother was addicted to sugar and her erratic behavior made us kids run for cover when we sensed she was in one of her "moods." If she wasn't depressed and asleep, she was screaming and ranting about what we did or hadn't done. Some days I just wanted to run away from home.*
>
> —*Tanya, twenty-four*

Recommended reading:

Lick the Sugar Habit, by Nancy Appleton, Avery Press, Garden City Park, NY, 1988.

Sugar Blues, by William Duffy, Warner Books, NY, 1975.

Other Addictive Drugs

The use of amphetamines, depressants, psychedelics, opiates, and the new rage, anabolic steroids, takes us out of ourselves and makes us incapable of thinking in FamilyMind. Unable to relate effectively to others, family members who use heavy drugs become isolated. The addict becomes lost, always on the taking side of give'ntake, making meaningful family interaction impossible. The healthy development of the family comes to a halt, interrupted by an insidious drain on finances, trust, cooperation, participation, presence, and really, really needs. The addicted member falls into a black hole that sucks the life out of the addict and the family group.

> *My cousin became addicted to heroin, then cocaine. He had been a successful dentist until he lost his practice, his family, and his home. Life got so scary for his wife that she took the kids and left. He's now living with his brother in some shack in the country where they live the drugged-out lifestyle. I don't suppose he'll live long enough to be an old man.*
>
> *—Samson, thirty-six*

Networks:

National Drug Hotline of the National Institute on Drug Abuse (800) 662-HELP

Nar-Anon Family Groups World Service Office
P.O. Box 2562
Palos Verdes, CA 90274
(310) 547-5800

Recommended reading:

Request reading materials from World Services Office, (310) 547-5800.

Sadly, when parents use drugs and other substances, their children are likely to do the same. A child with one alcoholic parent is 34 percent more likely to abuse alcohol than a child of nonalcoholics. A child is 400 percent more likely to become a heavy drinker if both parents are alcoholic.[7] Over and over we see teens in trouble for drug use whose parents are also users. *Through our example,* our children either learn to use substances that keep them removed from their feelings, or they learn to cope with their feelings within the safe embrace of the give'ntake love of family life.

Endnotes: Part Eight

1. Gail Sheehy, *Speed Is of the Essence* (New York: Pocket Books, 1971).

2. Pearl Bailey, as quoted in *The Quotable Woman* (Philadelphia: Running Press, 1991), 149.

3. Richard Kluger, *Ashes to Ashes* (New York: Alfred A. Knopf, 1996), 415-416.

4. Ibid., 500.

5. Ibid., xi.

6. Debra Waterhouse, *Why Women Need Chocolate* (New York: Hyperion, 1995).

7. Nancy Rubin, *Ask Me If I Care* (Berkeley, CA: Ten Speed Press, 1994), 253.

PART NINE

Brain Chemistry and Other Obstacles to FamilyMind

"What is real?" asked the Rabbit one day, when they were lying side by side....“Does it mean having things that buzz inside you and a stick out handle?” “Real isn’t how you are made,” said the Skin Horse. “It’s a thing that happens to you. When a child loves you for a long long time, not just to play with, but REALLY loves you, then you become real.” “Does it hurt?” asked the Rabbit. “Sometimes,” said the Skin Horse, for he was always truthful. “When you are Real you don’t mind being hurt.” “Does it happen all at once, like being wound up,” he asked “or bit by bit?” “It doesn’t happen all at once. You become. It takes a long time. That’s why it doesn’t often happen to people who break easily, or have sharp edges, or who have to be carefully kept. Generally, by the time you are Real, most of your hair has been loved off, and your eyes drop out and you get loose in the joints and very shabby. But these things don’t matter at all because once you are Real you can’t be ugly, except to people who don’t understand." [1]

—Margery Williams, *The Velveteen Rabbit*

ATTENTION: The purpose of this chapter is NOT to make diagnosis or to prescribe treatment. Our intent is to provide thumbnail sketches of some biochemical/psychological imbalances that may exist within ourselves and other family members that make FamilyMind difficult to use. When, no matter what we do, give'ntake love becomes really skewed in our family relationships, something deeper is happening, and being familiar with these obstacles will alert us to the need for outside education, consultation, and/or assistance. Keep in mind that the following descriptions are of disruptive behaviors and symptoms that a person cannot control simply by using willpower. People with these conditions often carry extreme guilt or shame because they cannot control their behaviors or symptoms, and these intense feelings often add to the general distress. Accurate diagnosis and treatment of these obstacles can mean "a new lease on life" for the sufferer and the entire family.

Soul Loss

In ancient cultures the shaman, or medicine man, performed the sacred rites of *soul retrieval* whenever a tribal member experienced a loss of power through depression or illness, because it was believed that a part of him or her had become lost.[2] This meant that the person afflicted could no longer live as a whole human being. Those of us who have experienced depression know the darkness we feel leaves no space for our active, hopeful, creative, joyful parts, and for a time they are completely lost to us. Without our whole selves, our personal power—the power to know what we want and need, the power to choose, the power to act, and so on—is diminished.

There are many symptoms of soul loss, such as physical illness, depression, and other biological and psychological disorders, that make being in a family group difficult, if not impossible. Perhaps we have tried different methods of soul retrieval, such as personal and family therapy, spiritual counseling, educational classes, prayer, inspirational reading, meditation, and so on. Ancient healing rituals of the shaman took many forms, as well. Often the shaman entered a trance-state that allowed him or her to "see" the cause of the afflicted person's soul loss and to "find" the effective healing cure.

We again make it clear that we do *not* prescribe healing cures in this chapter but offer instead descriptions of modern soul loss that commonly make it difficult to create a healthy family life. Keep in mind that the symptoms of these disorders appear in individuals in varying degrees. The fact that we or a family member have some or all of the symptoms described in the following paragraphs does not mean we, or they, have a certain psychological disorder or condition. Be assured that there is an amazing variety of human coping behaviors that help us deal with most life situations. For example, we all go in and out of FamilyMind thinking; occasionally, we overreceive; sometimes we overgive; most of us have experienced depression at some time in our lives; and we all get sick. However, if we have struggled for years with particularly difficult, stubborn, or painful response patterns that stay intact no matter what healing cure we try, the following descriptions may offer other "streets" to explore or other healing cures we have not thought of before.

Post Traumatic Stress Disorder

A Vietnam veteran who, after fifteen years, still wants to duck under the nearest car when a plane flies overhead is suffering from an extreme form of post traumatic stress. A father who becomes unusually angry when his child spills her milk, a mother who constantly cries over the simplest of things, or a young husband who continuously forgets things may all suffer from the effects of traumatic events that happened in their pasts. Past experiences that are too painful to cope with are stored in compartments within the brain and live on within us. The fear or pain from these past events can be triggered by similar, present-day experiences, such as divorce, serious accident, death, serious illness, change of job, move of household, school problems, arguments, affairs, grown children leaving the nest, physical abuse, and so on. Until the emotional and physical effects of the original event are released and integrated, we remain at the mercy of the past. Many, many people in our culture suffer from post traumatic stress, because we do not know how or do not take the time to deal with the after-effects of sudden, critical changes in our lives. A man who was mugged in his twenties leaves lights on all over the house in his forties to make his home safe. A woman who suffered childhood sexual abuse reads compulsively in bed until the lights are out to ward off intimacy with her spouse. A man whose father had a violent temper does everything he can to please those around him in adulthood to protect himself from the possible disapproval and anger of others.

Post traumatic stress interferes with FamilyMind thinking, because the person has difficulty knowing and saying what he or she really needs. Needs become unconsciously linked to the trauma of the past, and old feelings of fear, anxiety, or anger are triggered. For example, a person may say she needs to be held, but when her mate holds her, she becomes angry. She may have been hurt in her childhood by a parent she was close to, and pain and closeness got stored in the same compartment. When the person realizes that she really needs to feel safe first, then closeness and pain become separated, and the woman is more likely to be able to be close to her mate. When other family members try to relate to a person with post traumatic stress, they often experience pain and arguments, because the sufferer often *says* he needs one thing, only to find that he really needs something else.

> *I was very ambivalent about becoming a father. I told my wife that I would want her to be in charge of most of the parenting. I wanted to be free to pursue my career and not be bogged down with family needs. When she followed through on my request and took over parenting responsibilities, I became enraged. I felt alone, left out, and betrayed. It wasn't until I traced my feelings back to my own childhood with a father who didn't want to have any part of my care, that I realized where my conflict came from.*
>
> —*Lyle, thirty-two*

Psychotherapy, especially using an approach called Eye Movement Desensitization and Reprocessing, is effective when the emotions and memory that were stored in special compartments of the brain are brought to conscious awareness. The trauma is no longer hidden and will not be triggered by current events, allowing the person to respond to his or her own and others' needs in the present moment.

Networks:

EMDR Institute, Inc.
P.O. Box 1010
Pacific Grove, CA 93950
(408) 372-3900

National Council on Child Abuse and Family Violence Help Line
(800) 222-2000

Recommended reading:

Eye Movement Desensitization and Reprocessing, by Francine Shapiro, The Guilford Press, New York, 1995.

Post Traumatic Stress Disorder: The Victim's Guide, by Raymond B. Flannery, Jr., Ph.D., Continuum, New York, 1992.

The Courage to Heal: A Guide for Women Survivors of Child Sexual Abuse, by Ellen Bass and Laura Davis, Harper & Row, New York, 1988.

Dissociation

Dissociation is an extreme form of Post Traumatic Stress Disorder. In this instance, the past trauma suffered was so great that to survive, a person had to emotionally and psychologically disconnect from the pain and block all or some of the experience from current memory. Possible traumas include childhood sexual, emotional, and physical abuse and situations involving life or death, real or perceived. The following symptoms may signal dissociation:

- blanking out parts of conversations and events, because they trigger the memory of the past

- having the feeling of standing outside and watching oneself relate and act as though someone else has taken over
- feeling over-sensitive or under-sensitive to touch and emotional closeness
- feeling emotionally numb

Dissociation gets in the way of FamilyMind interaction by rendering a person unable to verbalize his or her needs. Because he or she has withdrawn from intense feelings, the dissociative is out of touch with the moment and unable to be emotionally present. Most people with dissociation cope by living from "shoulds," "ought to's," and strict role expectations. Other family members feel controlled, ignored, or that they are groping in the dark trying to make contact to understand what is really going on. This extreme form of PTSD is most troublesome in FamilyMind, because the person often cannot remember parts of arguments and agreements, genuinely disbelieving they said or agreed to such a thing. This behavior is very subtle and confusing to everyone involved.

Networks:

The International Society for the Study of Dissociation
4700 West Lake Avenue
Glenview, IL 60025-1485
(708) 375-4718

Childhelp/IOF Foresters National Child Abuse Hotline
(800) 4-A-CHILD

Recommended reading:

Ritual Abuse, by Margaret Smith, Harper San Francisco, 1993.

Uncovering the Mystery of MPD, by James G. Friesen, Ph.D., Thomas Nelson, Inc., Nashville, TN, 1991.

The Mosaic Mind, by Regina A. Goulding and Richard C. Schwartz, W.W. Norton and Company, New York, 1995.

Attention Deficit Disorder

ADD occurs in both children and adults, women and men, and is caused by an underactive frontal-orbital cortex of the brain. This cortex is nicknamed the "Executive Sorter," and its weakness can cause the following symptoms:

- short attention span

- tendency to start many tasks and projects well but seldom finish

- impulsivity—acting before thinking

- inability to connect to the big picture

- difficulty with order and prioritization

- tendency to get lost in fantasy

- hyperactivity

- seeks immediate gratification of needs

People with ADD suffer the above symptoms in varying degrees, but most tend to draw negative attention because of their inability to complete tasks and follow through on agreements made. They *intend* to finish that project and they *mean* to keep their agreements, but they are easily distracted. People with ADD often dominate the family group, either directly or indirectly, because the havoc they create usually results in arguments and fighting. Because they have difficulty maintaining a focus on the needs of others, and because their own perceptions change so quickly, they are unreliable a particular cause for concern when the sufferer is a parent.

Understanding of this biochemical problem has increased tremendously in recent years, and effective treatment therapies and medications have been developed. We caution that people can have some of the symptoms of ADD without the disorder. Testing by a trained clinician is the sure way to diagnose it and to form an individual treatment plan. An effective plan will include simplifying the lifestyle, learning to complete tasks one by one, establishing a structure with simple, regular routines, using lists, working with a coach who can offer suggestions the ADD sufferer had not thought of, and often medication.

> *I change so quickly from one thing to the next, and it confuses my children. One minute I set a consequence of no TV because their grades are bad. Then later that night, I'd go get a video to calm them down so I didn't feel so overwhelmed. I forget little things like where my keys are, appointment times, my purse, and directions. I have trouble completing things. My family calls me "ditzy but kind." When I get angry, I start planning to leave my husband, and when I calm down I decide not to. When my new counselor described ADD symptoms, I felt like he was looking into my mind and my life of thirty-six years. I decided that since my children depend on me so much, I should try the medication. For the first time in my life I actually complete tasks around the house, and I'm more consistent with my children. I forget less and feel much, much calmer. I still have my old habits of wanting to change or move away from things I feel overwhelmed by, but I feel less driven to do it. My kids think they have a new mom, especially when I follow through on consequences. It hurts when I think about how this has affected my kids. But I am so relieved.*
>
> *—Shannon, thirty-five*

> *I constantly think about baseball. I'm forty-three years old, and I still fantasize about playing outfield for the Cubs. At home, I can't sit still, always having to mow the yard, fix the car, clean the house, or fiddle on the computer. But worse, I start so many projects and hardly ever finish any of them well. My wife threatens to bulldoze the place every month. I was diagnosed with ADHD as a child. I could never sit still long enough to complete school, so I got my GED after I started taking the medication for ADD. After I got my degree and was*

in my twenties, I stopped the meds and figured I had outgrown my problem. Now as new ADHD info is coming out for adults, I read an article and realized I hadn't grown out of it. I just work around it. I had to admit I had a problem I would live with forever and start taking the meds again. This time I needed a smaller dose. I'm more focused all around, especially at home. I can now sit with my family and hang out on weekends. It's like I am getting to know them for the first time and getting to know myself again. I still like the Cubs, but I am not as obsessed as I was and I realize that a forty-three-year-old man is not going to be able to play their outfield. I can help my nine-year-old play his.

—Kurt, forty-three

Networks:

AADF (Adult Attention Deficit Foundation)
132 North Woodward Avenue
Birmingham, MI 48009
(313) 540-6335

Recommended reading:

Driven to Distraction, by E. Hallowell and J. Ratey, Pantheon Books, New York, 1994.

You Mean I'm Not Lazy, Stupid, or Crazy?!, by K. Kelly and P. Ramundo, Simon and Schuster, New York, 1993.

Obsessive Compulsive Disorder

The obsessive component of this disorder involves being unable to stop thinking and worrying about things; the compulsive part needs to have control over things in a certain way. These needs show themselves as perfectionism, inflexibility, and dictatorial behavior. Obsessive-compulsive people are intent on controlling everything and everyone around them to contain their enormous fears and anxieties. The external order of things holds much more importance than the internal awareness of needs.

> *My mother was frantic to look good to the neighbors, other family, everyone. She always wrote "thank you" notes after being a guest at someone's house for dinner and for holiday and birthday gifts. It wasn't so much that she was thankful, it was just the proper thing to do.*
>
> *—Riki, twenty-five*

The obsessive-compulsive person's challenge to being in FamilyMind is that he or she lives from "shoulds" and "ought to's," rather than from what she or he and the family really, really need. These families look good on the outside, but inside the relationships between members are usually marked by anger, depression, and distance. They often find themselves just "going through the motions" to get through another day.

Because OCD is a biochemical disorder, medications from the Prozac family of drugs are often helpful in reducing the obsessive and compulsive behaviors. Therapies that focus on a gradual awareness of real emotions and feelings enable people with OCD to be more present within their families, more in tune with their needs and the needs of others.

Networks:

Obsessive Compulsive Foundation (OC Foundation)
P.O. Box 9673
New Haven, CT 06535
(203) 772-0565

Recommended reading:

The Boy Who Couldn't Stop Washing, by Judith Rappoport, M.D., E.P. Dutton, New York, 1989.

Obsessive-Compulsive Disorders, by Steven Levenkron, Warner Books, New York, 1991.

Chronic Depression

Short-term depression is a grief response to a traumatic loss: the death of a loved one, a divorce, or loss of a job. As the name implies, this kind of depression does end after a time. Chronic depression is a long-term condition, seemingly without end, with varying degrees of sadness, hopelessness, and powerlessness. With chronic depression we lose a connection with the self and feel unable to cope with the basics of life. "I *can't* see a light at the end of the tunnel," depressed clients often say.

A chronically depressed family member, unable to experience joy or spontaneity, becomes a weight on the family. Other family members long to come to the rescue and usually end up feeling helpless or guilty. Children, especially, may feel responsible for a depressed parent's emotional state. Because suicidal thoughts, feelings, and sometimes actions are a danger, FamilyMind becomes skewed to the overgiving side of the relationship, and feelings of resentment, jealousy, and a general anxiety pervade the home atmosphere. Walking on eggshells is hard on everyone and leaves the family feeling drained and listless or hyper and agitated. *It is essential to get help.* Long-term psycho-therapy can refocus our feelings, reconnect us to our passions, and rekindle our feelings of hope about living.

Networks:

Depression and Related Affective Disorders Association (DRADA)
John Hopkins University School of Medicine
Meyer 3-181
600 N. Wolfe Street
Baltimore, MD 21287
(410) 955-4647

American Association of Suicidology
2459 South Ash
Denver, CO 80222
(303) 692-0985

Recommended reading:

Listening to Prozac, by Peter D. Kramer, M.D., Penguin, New York, 1993.

Waking Up Alive, by Richard A. Heckler, Ph.D., G.P. Putnam's Sons, New York, 1994.

Anxieties/Phobias

People with unrealistic fears and worries in their current lives are often reacting to traumatic events that happened in their past. Some common phobias include a fear of crossing bridges, of going through tunnels, of flying, of leaving one's home, of earthquakes or other natural disasters, and of riding in a car. Many of us may question how common these phobias are, and the truth is that they are very, very common. Most sufferers can "white knuckle" their way through, until the fear is overwhelmingly heightened by a life stressor, such as illness, divorce, loss of job, or death of a loved one. Then their lives can become homebound and dependent. Family members compensate by rearranging household routines that revolve around the phobia, and life becomes more complicated for everyone.

> *I've had a fear of crossing bridges for years, and one day during EMDR treatment, I remembered falling off the roof into our swimming pool and hitting my head. I relived the feeling that I was going to die, and I've had the same feeling ever since whenever I had to cross a bridge.*
>
> *—Ed, forty-five*

Treatment involves a gradual desensitizing of the anxiety connected with the event along with the emotional realization that the original trauma is over. The Eye Movement Desensitization and Reprocessing mentioned earlier is especially helpful for dispelling anxieties and phobias. Some therapists work more effectively with phobias *in vivo*. For example, Charles Wickstrad, a marriage, family, and child counselor in Alameda, California, works with clients that have a fear of flying in cooperation with a local airline. After several office sessions of EMDR, Charles and his client fly to Los Angeles for a meal and a return flight to celebrate the victory over the phobia.[3]

Networks:

Anxiety Disorders Association of America
6000 Executive Boulevard, Suite 513
Rockville, MD 20852
(301) 231-9350

National Institute of Mental Health
(800) 64-PANIC

Anxiety Disorders Resource Center
Third Floor, 79 Madison Avenue
New York, NY 10016 (212) 213-0909

Recommended reading:

Don't Panic, by R. Reid Wilson, Harper & Row, New York, 1986.

Anxiety Disorders and Phobias, by Aaron Beck and Gary Emery, Basic Books, New York, 1985.

Premenstrual Syndrome

Premenstrual syndrome or PMS, is a collection of symptoms that afflict many women ten to fourteen days before, and sometimes after, the onset of menstruation. As many as ten to fourteen million American women between twenty and fifty suffer some symptoms of PMS every month,[4] and the list of symptoms is huge. Some of the more common ones are:

irritability	asthma
acne	fainting
anxiety	breast tenderness and swelling
boils	tremulousness
mood swings	rhinitis

allergies

depression

hives

hostility

cystitis

migraine

urethritis

headache

less frequent urination

dizziness

abdominal bloating

sore throat

weight gain

hoarseness

constipation

joint pain and swelling

sugar/chocolate craving

backache

cramps [5]

Women who experience PMS often suffer five or more of these symptoms. It affects their work lives, personal and familial relationships, and how they feel about themselves both physically and emotionally. The extreme rage some women experience is enough for some husbands to dive for the nearest bomb shelter. The feelings of vulnerability for other women are so strong they want to cocoon themselves in a dark room under a cozy quilt until the period passes. In ancient cultures, women retreated to a quiet sanctuary to be ministered to by other women away from the activities of daily life.

Every month I was visited by a demon witch. I felt as though she took over my body and did things I would never ordinarily do. Fits of rage, throwing things in anger, hitting my husband—this wasn't really me. After my period started, I was myself again, and I spent a lot of time cleaning up the pieces of my family's hurt feelings and fear.

—Joanne, forty

I get so sick before my period with nausea, swelling in my hands and feet, dull ache in my middle back, and breasts so sore I cry out if anyone bumps me. You can imagine how my husband feels for three weeks out of every month—I don't want him to come near me! Our marriage is really falling apart, and I can't get any relief from my symptoms. My doctor says I need to stop eating chocolate, but that's the only thing that makes me feel better.

—*Ada, twenty-six*

I am so tired right before my period I have to drag myself around. I don't want to cook; I don't want to shop; I don't want to deal with kids. Please just let me sit and drink tea with my friends in a warm, cozy spot, and I'll be fine until this passes.

—*Jeanne, forty-eight*

I thought my allergies and asthma were a chronic thing until I learned that they can be symptoms of PMS. So, I kept track of my attacks and just like clockwork, I came down every month two weeks before my period with a sore throat, sinus pain, and wheezing. During those days I wish I didn't have a body!

—*Linda, thirty-two*

For many years the Western medical profession believed that premenstrual symptoms were a natural part of a woman's cycle, or worse, that they were "all in her head." The best doctors could do was to prescribe birth control pills, diuretics, antidepressants, and pain killers. She—and her family—would just have to learn to live with the rest. We now know that PMS is generally hormonal in origin. Thanks to some pioneering women doctors who themselves suffered monthly PMS symptoms, effective treatments and remedies have been discovered and developed. Acupuncture, vitamin therapy, exercise, stress reduction techniques, and an appropriate diet have all proved beneficial for relieving the symptoms of PMS.

Sometimes, simply understanding what's happening to their bodies can help women and their families learn to deal with their needs during this time. Some women are relieved when their husbands remind them that "it's time," while others interpret a reminder as an accusation and become furious at the slightest mention. Each couple has to work it out for themselves, but many find that keeping track of a woman's cycle helps everyone know "where they are." Most of all, women want their feelings—both physical and emotional—to be validated. The men in their lives need to understand that what they experience is real, to respect the intensity of these feelings and symptoms, and to give the support and the space to deal with them.

Other cultures believe that the window to a woman's soul opens during ovulation and menstruation, causing a general vulnerability at these times. Some women are more susceptible to relapses of certain cyclical illness, such as Epstein-Barr, allergies, lupus, and chronic fatigue syndrome.[6]

A note of caution about PMS: The tendency to blame all conflict within a family on the woman's PMS is dangerous, dishonest, and unjust.

⇘ *JEANNE* | Don and I find that when I'm feeling irritable or angry before my period, he often "rises to the occasion" by coming back at me with anger. *Then* the conflict happens. I may start it, but he escalates it. One thing that helps is for us both to realize that I'm under the control of my hormones, and Don's responses carry a great impact. When he can respond to my sharpness with "Ouch! I feel hurt," or "Do I need to head for cover?" or "Tell me more about that," I am reminded of where I am and who he is. Asking the FamilyMind Question, "What do we need now, *including me*?" helps us get through these touchy days without too many scars.

Networks:

The PMS Self Help Center
101 First Street, Suite 441
Los Altos, CA 94022
(415) 964-7268

Womankind
P.O. Box 1775
Sebastopol, CA 95473
(707) 522-8662

Recommended reading:

PMS: Premenstrual Syndrome Self Help Book, by Susan M. Lark, M.D., Celestial Arts, Berkeley, CA, 1984.

The Wise Wound: Myths, Realities, and Meanings of Menstruation, by Penelope Shuttle and Peter Redgrove, Bantam Books, New York, 1978.

Reclaiming the Menstrual Matrix, by Tamara Slayton. Available exclusively from Womankind Publishing, P.O. Box 1775, Sebastopol, CA, 95473, 1995.

Child-Specific Difficulties

There are conditions of childhood that greatly diminish a child's ability to be an active member of a family. We mention them briefly here so that a physician or counselor can be consulted if any of the symptoms sound familiar. Again, we do not intend to offer in-depth descriptions, diagnosis, or treatment plans. One of a parent's greatest concerns for their child with difficulties is that he or she will become overly dependent, narcissistic, and problem-focused because of the special circumstances the disability creates within the family. The FamilyMind Question helps families keep individual needs in perspective, while guiding the child to give and receive according to his or her capabilities.

Asthma and Allergies

The onset of these illnesses can occur anytime and often appear in young children with the symptoms of runny or stuffed up nose, skin irritations, coughing, wheezing, stomach cramps, sore throat, as well as attention and behavioral problems. Airborne allergens, including animal dander, dust mites, pollens, and molds, are most common, along with certain foods, vitamins, medicines, fabrics, insect bites, and household cleaning products. Over time an allergy or asthma sufferer may experience chronic fatigue, loss of appetite, and a suppressed immune system, rendering them more susceptible to colds, bronchitis, and flu. A child who has chronic allergies or asthma does not feel well and has little energy to give to family relationships; sometimes they can just manage to breathe. There are many medications and natural remedies for allergy and asthma sufferers. Often a combination of methods, from clearing the home environment of suspected allergens to allergy injections, bring needed relief. Ask a pediatrician for a referral to a local allergy specialist or check the following resources:

Networks:

Asthma and Allergy Foundation of America
1125 15th. Avenue, N.W., Suite 502
Washington, D.C. 20005
(202) 466-7643
(800) 7-ASTHMA

Real Goods Catalog
555 Leslie Street
Ukiah, CA 95488-5576
(800) 762-7325

Recommended reading:

Children with Asthma: A Manual for Parents, by Thomas F. Plaut, M.D., 2nd ed., Pedipress, Amherst, MA, 1988.

The Best Guide to Allergy, by Schultz, M.D., Giannini, M.D., Chang, M.D., and Wong, M.D., 3rd ed., Humona Press, Totowa, NY, 1994.

Attention Deficit Hyperactive Disorder

ADD in children is often accompanied by hyperactivity, therefore the name ADHD. Children with ADHD can be dreamy, spacy, forgetful, and inattentive. They may have difficulty making transitions from one activity to the next, they may act out at home, and they may have behavioral problems at school. Girls especially get stuck in emotionality, crying endlessly over a small slight or hurt. Boys tend toward hyperactivity—hitting, fighting, perpetually in motion.

Families with a child with ADHD are in constant turmoil, never knowing what to expect. Routine tasks, such as teeth brushing, getting ready for school, and doing simple chores can reach nightmarish proportions, because the child has difficulty staying on tasks and completing them. Parents find themselves repeating directions over and over, often ending in frustration and anger.

My self is fine. It's just my brain that's screwed up!

—Cal, sixteen

Testing by a trained clinician to confirm an ADHD diagnosis is crucial to developing a treatment plan. Children with ADHD respond well to firm routines so they know what to expect throughout the day. For example, rising and bedtime rituals that are done each day are reassuring and comforting. The combination of regular patterns of sleep, the reduction or elimination of television watching and computer use, alternating cycles of motion and rest, such as ten minutes of studying spelling words and fifteen minutes of playing catch with Mom or Dad, and medication, makes an effective treatment plan.

Many people are hesitant to put their children on medication when they are very young. We share that concern. Other parts of the treatment plan can offer much relief. However, children with ADHD are so often labeled lazy, stupid, or a behavioral problem, which leads to feelings of shame and low self-esteem. These children are usually very intelligent and talented, and a treatment that helps them develop beyond the restrictions of their biochemical imbalance is crucial.

When I was in the third grade other kids didn't like me,
because I sometimes pushed them too hard on the

playground. I didn't want to hurt anybody, but the teachers got real mad. They didn't like for me to get out of my seat, either, but I just couldn't help it. If I didn't move, I thought I would explode! Now I'm in the fifth grade, and this teacher is really nice. She puts me in the front row, not the back, and she pats me alot on the shoulder. We have an agreement that if I can't sit still, I raise two fingers, and I can go get a drink of water. My mom and dad are a lot happier that I don't get in trouble so much. They were tired of talking to the principal all the time. I have friends, too!

—Jimmy, eleven

Networks:

C.H.A.D.D. (Children with Attention Deficit Disorders)
1859 North Pine Island Road, Suite 185
Plantation, FL 33322
(305) 587-3700

Recommended reading:

Raising a Son: Parents and the Making of a Healthy Man, by Don and Jeanne Elium, Celestial Arts, Berkeley, CA, rev. ed. 1996.

Raising Your Spirited Child, by Mary Sheedy Kurcinka, Harper Perennial, New York, 1992.

Autism

This neurological disorder involves a number of symptoms that many children may experience at some time during their development. It is, therefore, somewhat difficult to diagnose until a number of clearly seen patterns emerge. These include a response to the environment that is out of the ordinary, such as an extremely frightened reaction to being touched or no reaction at all to a loud noise. Most autistic children have problems with language development and in expressing themselves. They have difficulty playing with other children and seem confused by the normal behavior of others. They may participate in unusual play activities that become annoying or obsessive, such as continuous rocking, twirling, monotonous humming, or pounding objects together. A child with autism usually shows an uneven developmental pattern, advanced in some areas, but far behind in others. For example, one child may know the names of most dinosaurs but have difficulty building a block tower. Another may be dexterous at puzzles and drawing but fail to be toilet-trained by age four. Because of this discrepancy in development, it is difficult for parents to know and remember what their child really needs. For most autistic children it is extremely difficult to develop successful relationships within the family. Odd behaviors like head-banging and grimacing make it hard to know how to respond. New research has contributed to the development of treatment for this disorder, and most experts in the field recommend joining a national organization for support and information on the latest therapies. Correct diagnosis and education help parents know how to meet their child's needs. This is especially important in less severe cases where behaviors are attributed to stubbornness, lack of intelligence, or a character flaw, rather than autism.

Networks:

Autism Society of America
7910 Woodmont Avenue, Suite 650
Bethesda, MD 20814
(800) 328-8476

Recommended Reading:

The Siege, by Clara Claiborn Park, Harcourt, Brace, and World, New York, 1967.

A Parent's Guide To Autism, by Charles A. Hart, Pocket Books, New York, 1993.

Son-Rise, by Barry Neil Kaufman, Warner Books, New York, 1976.

Dyslexia

The symptoms of dyslexia manifest as disorientation that mainly affects the senses of hearing, vision, time, balance, and movement. Children with this disorder suffer different distortions. For example, letters or numbers may appear reversed or changed; spelling is often poor; and a reader with dyslexia may skip words or lines. Some children with dyslexia have difficulty making certain speech sounds, such as "ch" or "th," and they may seem not to hear or listen well to what is said. They may experience dizziness or nausea when reading and have difficulty sitting still. These children are easily distracted, often lose their train of thought, and find math concepts and telling time hard to learn. They may be consistently late. To compensate for their difficulties some children develop habits that further affect their ability to learn, which may develop into behavioral problems both at school and at home.

Without appropriate treatment, the dyslexic child cannot fully participate within the family. Because most children with dyslexia have difficulty completing simple tasks, as well as trouble with reading and spelling, they tend to see themselves as failures. They may take on, and live up to, the role of the family "dummy" or "the difficult one." Real needs get lost in the role, and these children do not know how to ask for help. Effective treatment for dyslexia will help parents and other family members, as well as the afflicted child, understand the limitations that this disorder imposes and how to find out the child's real needs.

Networks:

Otton Dyslexia Society
8600 LaSalle Road, Chester Bldg., Suite 382
Baltimore, MD 21204
(800) ABC-D123

Recommended reading:

The Gift of Dyslexia, by Ronald D. Davis, Ability Workshop Press, San Juan Capistrano, CA, 1994.

You Don't Have to Be Dyslexic, by Joan Smith, Learning Times, Sacramento, CA, 1991.

Chronic Illness

Chronic illness in childhood, such as epilepsy, diabetes, heart ailments, and cancer, cause great distress and disruption in family life. It can drive a wedge into the best of marriages, as parents lose perspective on the family group while exhausting all their energies and resources on the illness. Siblings eventually feel left out and betrayed because of the necessary attention given to the sick brother or sister. The FamilyMind Question, "What do we all need, including me?" becomes vital, in spite of how hard it is to see to everyone's needs. The Question brings the attention back to center, where all family members are considered as needful and *deserving* of giving and receiving love.

Networks:

Association for the Care of Children's Health (ACCH)
7910 Woodmont Avenue, Suite 300
Bethesda, MD 20814
(301) 654-6549

Recommended reading:

Raising a Child Who Has a Physical Disability, by Donna Albrecht, John Wiley, New York, 1995.

Managing Your Child's Diabetes, by Johnson and Kleinman, Master Media, New York, 1995.

Manic Depressive Disorders

Manic depressive (or bipolar) disorders manifest differently in adults than in children. Adults tend toward more extreme highs and lows. Symptoms in childhood are cyclical, but children tend to present chronic agitation, irritation, and aggressiveness with a desire to hurt others that increases over time. Without treatment and medication, symptoms will only accelerate and tear a family apart. These children become out of control, go to foster or group homes, and often end up as members of violent gangs, and worse. Children with manic depressive disorder are a challenge for their families. We urge such families to do whatever it takes to find treatment and support for everyone.

Networks:

National Depressive and Manic-Depressive Association (NDMDA)
730 North Franklin Street, Suite 501
Chicago, IL 60610
(800) 826-3632

School and Other Phobias

Common phobias among children include:

ailurophobia - fear of cats

agoraphobia - fear of leaving home

arachnophobia - fear of spiders

arophobia - fear of heights

brontophobia - fear of thunder

claustrophobia - fear of small places

cynophobia - fear of dogs

dentist phobias

doctor phobias

entomophobia - fear of insects

hematophobia - fear of blood

mysophobia - fear of germs and dirt

nyctophobia - fear of dark

ophidophobia - fear of snakes

pyrophobia - fear of fire

xenophobia - fear of strangers

zoophobia - fear of animals

These fears in children should be taken seriously and treated early. Otherwise, family life bogs down while trying to avoid the subject of a child's phobia, schedules and routines become overly complicated, parents become exhausted, and the child suffers. It is tempting to try to normalize the abnormal situation of a phobia by joking about it, punishing it, or ignoring it. All too often these reactions only cause more distress and guilt in the child and threaten his or her trust in family relationships. Systematic desensitization and relaxation techniques are helpful in treating phobias, and the EMDR method described earlier is recommended.

Networks:

Anxiety Disorders Association of America
6000 Executive Boulevard, Suite 513
Rockville, MD 20852
(301) 231-9350

National Institute of Mental Health
(800) 64-PANIC

Recommended reading:

Feel the Fear and Do It Anyway, by S. Jeffers, Fawcett, New York, 1992.

Sleep Disorders

Having difficulty falling asleep, waking in the middle of the night, suffering nightmares and night terrors, apnea, bedwetting, and refusing to sleep in one's own bed are all common problems during childhood. They may begin at birth or develop during certain developmental growth stages. They may last for a short time or seem to go on and on forever. When a child has sleeping difficulties, the whole family goes into sleepwalking mode. Eventually, everyone is worn down to bare nerve endings; patience is easily lost; tempers flare;

giving and receiving falters; and family members stumble groggily through the day. There are many cures and treatments for sleep disorders including surgery and medication. Some cures may seem unorthodox, because they abandon cultural norms, like the family bed, for example, but we think that whatever it takes to get the family sleeping healthfully is worth trying.

Networks:

> The Stanford Sleeps Disorders Clinic
> 401 Quarry Way Rd. Ste. 3301A
> Stanford, CA 94305
> (415) 723-6601

Recommended reading:

> *Solve Your Child's Sleep Problems*, by Richard Ferber, M.D., Simon and Schuster, New York, 1986.

> *The Family Bed*, by Tine Thevenin, Avery Publishing Group, Wayne, New Jersey, 1987.

Tourette Syndrome

Most people have never heard of Tourette syndrome, and the exact cause of this brain disorder is not fully understood. It may develop gradually, giving the parents only a vague feeling that their child is somehow different from other children. Teachers may complain that he is inattentive, hyperactive, or difficult to control, but the family doctor may assume he is just going through a difficult phase and that there is nothing to worry about. Tourette syndrome (TS) may appear suddenly. Out of the blue, a child may develop odd body movements or make unusual sounds. These tics include twitching, blinking, humming, and throat clearing and tend to increase in frequency and number. To be diagnosed with TS, a child must have at least two motor tics and one vocal tic. What follows is a list of common repetitive and uncontrollable muscle movements in the body:

Motor tics:	Vocal tics:
finger movements	throat clearing
blinking eyes	sniffing
grimacing	coughing
kicking	grunting
sticking out tongue	spitting
jerking neck	yelling
eye rolling	animal sounds
biting	repeating words or phrases [7]
hitting	
touching	

Tourette syndrome is also associated with more bizarre, uncontrollable symptoms that include obscene gestures and language or self-injurious behaviors, such as hitting one's self, picking at scabs, and so on. Only a small percentage of children with this disorder suffer these symptoms.

A child with Tourette syndrome can be extremely disruptive in any environment. Dealing with the concern, embarrassment, and frustration the unusual symptoms often generate is quite taxing on parents and siblings, as well as the afflicted child. The symptoms can grow or diminish in number and severity, and change from facial grimacing to repeated animal sounds, for example. Just as the family has become accustomed to one set of symptoms, an entirely new set may emerge. A good treatment plan will involve the whole family with coaching on how to deal with the reactions of others, behavior management skills for the child with TS, as well as medication and educational therapies to help with the learning difficulties that often accompany this disorder. With skilled guidance from professionals a family can become more united and supportive of each other as a result of the special needs of a child with TS.

Networks:

Tourette Syndrome Association
42-40 Bell Blvd.
Bayside, NY 11361-2861
(800) 237-0717

American Association of University Affiliated Programs for
Persons with Developmental Disabilities (AAUAP)
8630 Fenton Street, Suite 410
Silver Spring, MD 20910
(301) 588-8252

Recommended reading:

Tourette Syndrome Association, Inc. Newsletter
42-40 Bell Blvd.
Bayside, NY 11361
(800) 237-0717

Children with Tourette Syndrome: A Parents' Guide, edited by Tracy
Haerle, Woodbine House, Bethesda, MD, 1992.

Weight Problems and Eating Disorders

Distortions in body image and eating problems afflict girls more
often than boys, and these disorders are occurring at a greater rate
and at younger ages than ever before. Boys who are overweight,
however, receive criticism and ridicule about their size; and boys who
aspire to be cyclists, skaters, wrestlers, or gymnasts are more at risk
of developing eating disorders to keep their weight within acceptable
limits.[8] With TV commercials, billboards, and magazine advertise-
ments, few children escape our zealous preoccupation with how we
look. Counting calories, restricting food intake, continuous dieting,
and concern about being fat by ten-year-olds can turn into bulimia
or anorexia by age eleven or twelve.

When food and eating become a power struggle between children
and parents, these issues lead to worry, guilt, frustration, and shame.
Family meals become battlefields, and family attention becomes focused

on who is eating, who is not eating, what is being eaten and on and on. The legacy of weight and eating disorders is tragic. Our children become so consumed by whether they measure up (or down) in outer appearance, that they lose touch with what matters on the inside. Effective treatment for anorexia, bulimia, and other eating disorders is available, and seeking help at the first sign of trouble is vital. Prolonged effects can be lethal. The clues that something may be wrong include the following:

- A weight gain or loss of ten to fifteen pounds within three to six weeks is a concern, unless there is a logical reason, such as an illness, a growth spurt, a body-building or athletics training program.

- An obsession with food, either eating it, or not eating it, can signal trouble.

- An emotional body image that does not match the physical reality leads, for example, to commenting on how fat or disgusting her body is while actually being within a normal body weight.

- An unrealistic body image that does not relate to her physical type or size leads to depression, self-criticism, and eating disorders.

- Sudden or frequent eating binges that the child cannot control may signal the beginning of a vicious cycle of bingeing, throwing up, the use of laxatives, and rigorous dieting to try to achieve or maintain what is, to the child, an acceptable body weight.

If any of these symptoms occur, get help from a pediatrician immediately. Of course, the best way to help our children develop good body images and healthy eating habits is to model this behavior for them—easier said than done. But, ensuring that all family members get a good night's sleep, regular exercise, plenty of fun, enough relaxation, and a variety of nourishing foods helps children learn through our example. It is the first line of defense to combat the messages from culture that we must look a certain way to be acceptable and loved.

Networks:

Anorexia Nervosa and Related Eating Disorders, Inc.
P.O. Box 5102
Eugene, OR 97405
(503) 344-1144

Shapedown Weight Management Program for Children
and Teens
Balboa Publishing
11 Library Place
San Anselmo, CA 94960
(415) 453-8886

Recommended reading:

Like Mother, Like Daughter, by Debra Waterhouse, Hyperion, New York, 1997.

Fat is a Family Affair, by Judi Hollis, Hazelton Foundation, Center City, MN, 1985.

Living With Anorexia and Bulimia, by James Morrey, St. Martin Press, New York, 1993.

Final Thoughts

The symptoms and behaviors of the disorders described here will sabotage our best efforts at using FamilyMind. It is important to note that high stress may intensify symptoms, making a family member's participation even more problematic. Major life traumas, such as divorce, the death of a loved one, or the loss of a job, may add another layer of symptoms or behaviors. Fortunately, treatment and support are available and an understanding of these "losses of soul" makes them easier to bear. We may be resistant to having our children tested for fear they will be labeled "ADD," "OCD," or "PTSD," and that these labels will follow them throughout their school careers and even their lives. To avoid pigeonholing people, it helps to see their disabilities as just a small part of who they truly are.

The success of medications, psychotherapy, and other treatments will vary from one individual to the next. What works for one person may not be the answer for another. We urge families to explore both traditional and alternative methods of treatment to find ways of healing that not only treat the body but speak to the soul. The following is a list of resources that offer complementary treatment alternatives:

Anthroposophical Medicine

Organizations:

North American Center for Anthroposophical Medicine (NACAM)
c/o Raphael House
7953 California Avenue
Fair Oaks, CA 95628

Recommended reading:

Home Remedies, by Otto Wolf, Anthroposophic Press, New York, 1991.

Caring for the Sick at Home, by Tineke van Bentheim, et. al., Floris Books, Edinburgh, 1980.

A Guide to Child Health, by Michaela Glöckler and Wolfgang Goebel, Floris Books, Edinburgh, 1984.

Lupus Novice, by Laura Chester, Station Hill Press, Barrytown, NY, 1989.

Traditional Healing Practices

Recommended reading:

The Four-Fold Way: Walking the Paths of the Warrior, Teacher, Healer, and Visionary, by Angeles Arrien, Ph.D., Harper San Francisco, 1993.

The Way of the Shaman: A Guide to Power and Healing, by Michael Harner, Bantam Books, New York, 1982.

Imagery and Healing: Shamanism and Modern Medicine, by Jeanne Achterberg, New Science Library, Boston, 1985.

Homeopathy

Organizations:

Homeopathic Educational Services
2124 Kittredge Street
Berkeley, CA 94704
(510) 649-0294 for information; (800) 359-9051 for orders

Recommended reading:

The Family Health Guide to Homeopathy, by Barry Rose, M.D., Celestial Arts, Berkeley, CA, 1992.

Chinese Medicine and Philosophy

Organizations:

American College of Traditional Chinese Medicine
455 Arkansas Street
San Francisco, CA 94107
(415) 282-7600

Feng Shui Network International
P.O. Box 2133
London W1A 1RL, United Kingdom
(0171) 935-8935

Recommended reading:

The Web That Has No Weaver, by Ted Kaptchuk, Contemporary Books, Inc., Chicago, 1984.

Acupressure for Common Ailments, by Chris Jarmey and John Tindal, Fireside Books, New York, 1991.

Feng Shui Made Easy, by William Spear, Harper San Francisco, 1995.

Diet and Nutrition

Organizations:

Earthsave Foundation
P.O. Box 949
Felton, CA 95018-0949
(408) 423-4069

North American Vegetarian Society
P.O. Box 72
Dolgeville, NY 13329
(518) 568-7970

Recommended reading:

Diet for a New America, by John Robbins, Stillpoint Publishing, Walpole, NH, 1987.

Gardening for Health and Nutrition, by John and Helen Philbrick, Anthroposophic Press, Hudson, NY, 1988.

Food and Mood, by Elizabeth Somer, M.A., R.D., Henry Holt and Co., New York, 1995.

The Moosewood Cookbook, by Mollie Katzen, Ten Speed Press, Berkeley, CA, 1992.

Secrets of the Soil, by Peter Tompkins and Christopher Bird, Harper and Row, New York, 1989.

Healthful Living

Organizations:

Center for the Study of Commercialism
1875 Connecticut Avenue, N.W., Suite 300
Washington, D.C. 20009-5728
(202) 332-9110

Recommended reading:

Voluntary Simplicity, by Duane Elgin, 2nd. ed., William Morrow, New York, 1993.

Beyond Prozac, by Michael, J. Norden, M.D., Regan Books, New York, 1995.

Plain and Simple: A Woman's Journey to the Amish by Sue Bender, HarperCollins, New York, 1989.

Kitchen Table Wisdom, by Rachel Naomi Remen, M.D., Riverhead Books, New York, 1996.

A Way in the World, by Ernest Boyer, Jr., Harper & Row, San Francisco, 1984.

Many readers may wonder why the following categories and resources are included in a book about making families work. In addition to considering individual members when we measure the health of a family, we must also view the whole family and its internal relationships. When we seek to improve the health of the body, we must also consider the health of the soul. Families cannot function independently of its members, and the condition of our souls influences the fitness of our bodies. "No man (or woman) is an island, entire of itself....", in poet John Donne's words. The books suggested here may lead to activities, experiences, and attitudes that invite a healing of both body and soul, heart and mind. We are reminded of the use of laughter by Norman Cousins to heal himself of cancer.[9] These resources are offered as supplements to conventional medical and psychological treatments and therapies.

Bibliotherapy, Myths, Archetypes, Poetry, and Stories

Recommended reading:

Revolution from Within: A Book of Self-Esteem, by Gloria Steinem, Little, Brown, and Company, Boston, 1992.

Women Who Run With the Wolves, by Clarissa Pinkola Estés, Ph.D., Ballantine Books, New York, 1992.

Goddesses in Everywoman, by Jean Shinoda Bolen, M.D., Harper Colophon Books, New York, 1984.

Gods in Everyman, by Jean Shinoda Bolen, M.D., Harper & Row, San Francisco, 1989.

Men and the Water of Life, by Michael Meade, Harper San Francisco, 1993.

Ritual

Recommended readings:

The Art of Ritual, by Renee Beck and Sydney Barbara Metrick, Celestial Arts, Berkeley, CA, 1990.

Grandmothers of the Light: A Medicine Woman's Sourcebook, by Paula Gunn Allen, Beacon Press, Boston, 1991.

To Dance with God, by Gertrud Mueller Nelson, Paulist Press, New York, 1986.

Creativity: Writing and Painting

Organizations:

John F. Kennedy University
Graduate School for Holistic Studies
Arts and Consciousness
12 Altarinda Road
Orinda, CA 94563
(510) 254-0105

Recommended reading:

At A Journal Workshop, by Ira Progoff, Dialogue House Library, New York, 1975.

Bird by Bird, by Anne Lamott, Pantheon Books, New York, 1994.

The Natural Way to Draw, by Kimon Nicolaïdes, Houghton Mifflin, Boston, 1969.

Painting with Children, by Brunhild Müller, Floris Books, Edinburgh, 1986.

The Artist's Way, by Julia Cameron, G.P. Putnam's Sons, New York, 1992.

Movement and Meditation

Organizations:

Transcendental Meditation Program
(800) 888-5797

Recommended reading:

The Serpent and the Wave, by Jalaja Bonheim, Celestial Arts, Berkeley, CA, 1992.

Embrace Tiger, Return to Mountain, by Al Chung-liang Huang, Celestial Arts, Berkeley, CA, 1987.

How to Meditate, by Lawrence LeShan, Bantam Books, New York, 1981.

Peace Is Every Step: The Path of Mindfulness in Everyday Life, by Thich Nhat Hanh, Bantam Books, New York, 1991.

The following section is offered for individuals or parents of children living with a chronic or life-threatening illness.

Spiritual Living and Dying

Organizations:

Center for Attitudinal Healing
19 Main Street
Tiburon, CA 94920
(415) 252-1666

Rigpa
P.O. Box 7866
Berkeley, CA 94707
(510) 644-3922

Commonweal Cancer Help Program
P.O. Box 316
Bolinas, CA 94924
(415) 868-0970

Recommended reading:

When Bad Things Happen to Good People, by Harold S. Kusher, Avon Books, New York, 1983.

The Tibetan Book of Living and Dying, by Sogyal Rinpoche, Harper San Francisco, 1992.

Who Dies, by Stephen Levine, Anchor Books, Garden City, NY, 1982.

On Death and Dying, by Elizabeth Kübler-Ross, Macmillan, Old Tappan, NJ, 1991.

Letters from the Light, written through the hand of Elsa Barker, Beyond Words, Hillsboro, OR, 1995.

The Eagle and the Rose, by Rosemary Altea, Warner Books, New York, 1995.

Ask Your Angels, by Alma Daniel, Timothy Wyllie, and Andrew Ramer, Ballantine Books, New York, 1992.

> *In those moments of despair...*
>
> *when I really don't care*
>
> *whether or not I survive,*
>
> *then, am I most keenly aware*
>
> *of the certainty that I will.*
>
> *That's the pain of it...*
>
> *and the miracle.*[10]
>
> —Portia Nelson,
> *There's a Hole in My Sidewalk*

Endnotes: Part Nine

1. Margery Williams, *The Velveteen Rabbit* (New York: Doubleday, Doran, 1922).

2. Sandra Ingerman, *Soul Retrieval: Mending the Fragmented Self* (San Francisco: Harper San Francisco, 1991).

3. Charles Wickstrad, M.F.C.C., in a conversation with Don Elium, Alameda, CA, 15 October 1996.

4. Susan M. Lark, *PMS: Self Help Book* (Berkeley, CA: Celestial Arts, 1984), 19.

5. Ibid., 20.

6. Laura Kennedy, anthroposophist, in a conversation with Jeanne Elium giving information from Christa van Tellingen, M.D., Anthroposophical medicine, Fair Oaks, CA, 20 June 1996.

7. Tracy Haerle, ed., *Children With Tourette Syndrome* (Rockville, MD: Woodbine House, 1992), 4.

8. Debra Waterhouse, author of *Outsmarting the Female Fat Cell, Why Women Need Chocolate*, and *Like Mother, Like Daughter* in a phone conversation with Jeanne Elium, Walnut Creek, CA, 5 November 1996.

9. Norman Cousins, *Anatomy of an Illness* (New York: Norton, 1979).

10. Portia Nelson, *There's a Hole in My Sidewalk: The Romance of Self-Discovery* (Hillsboro, OR: Beyond Words, 1993).

PART TEN

Children and FamilyMind— Growing Up

What we learn within the family are the most unforgettable lessons that our lives will ever teach us.[1]

—Maggie Scarf, *Intimate Worlds*

We cannot teach our children FamilyMind. They learn it by living it through our leadership and guidance. The degree to which they are able to be active family members depends upon their levels of growth and maturity. Philosopher, writer, and teacher Rudolf Steiner noted three, clear stages of childhood: the years from birth to seven when growth is body-centered; prepuberty when growth is preparing for the feeling life; and adolescence when the intellect comes into full bloom.[2] We call these years the willing, feeling, and thinking years, and their developmental stages bring unique challenges and needs to the family group. Understanding our children's stages of development helps us to help them participate within the family according to their growing capabilities. We realize that our toddler cannot be in charge of a family dinner, and we foresee that our teen may no longer want the usual party hats, cake, and ice cream birthday party. Our ten-year-old may still break down under too many expectations, and our college graduate may need new guidelines concerning household chores. How active any of us are in supporting family life depends upon our ages, emotional maturity, state of health, career and school demands, family expectations, and level of commitment. The intent of this chapter is not to teach discipline with punishments and rewards, but to describe our parental roles as leaders and guides for our children's participation in this family and in their future families.

The Willing Years

The willing years from birth to seven are the most demanding on parents to provide physical care. Babies and toddlers need twenty-four hour attention from someone with boundless love, endless patience, and tenacious attention for detail. During these years, the family group is geared toward setting physical limits and boundaries to provide safety, security, and space enough for little bodies to test the world. The outstanding code words for the willing years are *protection*, *action*, and *presence*. Babies to seven-year-olds must have the protection of the family group to survive. The family provides love, food, clothing, shelter, protection from illness, stimulation, a refuge from overstimulation, and safekeeping from the trauma of neglect, abandonment, incest, and physical and emotional abuse. Of great importance during the willing years are opportunities to strengthen the child's will nature. The will is linked with the instinct to grow, to develop, to master, and with the unconscious urge we see in the young child to practice a new skill over and over again until it is perfected. Our children achieve mastery over their bodies and surrounding environments through persistence, determination, and practice.

> *I watched my three-year-old grandson play happily for a solid hour in a dishpan of water and soapsuds. I, and the screened-in porch where we were sitting, ceased to exist for him, as he endlessly poured one cupful of water into another, watching the bubbles trickle over the edges of the cups, his hands, the dishpan. By some instinct of will, he unconsciously practiced pouring, becoming one with the water, the bubbles, the motion of dipping.*
>
> —*Alicia, sixty-four*

Toddlers ignite families to action through their insatiable desire to know about their environments. Everything comes under the scrutiny of the senses: *Look* what I found! What does it *feel* like? What does it *taste* like? Does it have a *smell?* If I shake it, does it make a *sound?* Never again will our children require as much of our presence in their lives. The mantra, "On your feet, Mom!" "On your feet, Dad!" carries us through our toddler's never-ending exploration and testing of the world and self. As she goes from one fascinating thing to the next, like a little butterfly drinking in precious nectar, we follow in her wake, reminding ("The stove is hot!"), explaining ("This belongs to your big sister."), distracting ("Here is *your* toy."), and teaching ("Let's do it this way."). If those of us who go out into the world to work think that parents who stay at home as caretakers of their children sit around and do nothing all day, just try following a two-year-old through her daily routine. It provides as much physical exercise as any personal trainer could devise and also taxes the emotions!

Focus of Development

Between birth and the time a child loses his first teeth, usually around age seven, growth is focused in the arms, legs, and the exercise of the will. The development of the body and the will are on the "front burners" of growth. On the "back burners" are the maturation of feelings and the development of the intellect. In other words, during these years, children are literally learning to control their bodies and actions, while control of feelings, cognitive thinking, and intellectual understanding wait in the background. The progression from sitting up to crawling to standing to walking upright alone are tremendous achievements in the early lives of our children, and they spend most of their waking hours working to accomplish these enormous tasks. Bladder and bowel control and the building of a tall tower of blocks are feats that call for real celebration. Making a ball bounce and watching food fall from the highchair to see what it does when it hits the floor are endlessly repeated to confirm the permanence of things and consistency of actions. Thinking and reasoning abilities are quite limited, the child feels a global connection to everything in his world, and he is prepared to love his caregivers with a devotion so deep that he carefully imitates all we do.

During the willing years, family life is centered around the physical—making the home environment safe, providing opportunities for play that involve running, climbing, jumping, and meeting the child's physical and emotional needs for love and attention. The needs of a child in the willing years seem disproportionate to the needs of the adults or older siblings. The family is by necessity "small-child" centered, and parents may at times feel burned out, overwhelmed, tired, resentful, angry, and even desperate. Time and energy for anything else but parenting a little one seem nonexistent.

"Sam had strained carrots again tonight.

Big huge mess, carrots everywhere, all over the kitty who

passed by at a bad time, on Sam's socks, in his hair, in my hair.

I can see that things are going to begin deteriorating

around here rather rapidly." [3]

—Anne Lamott, *Operating Instructions*

How To's and How Not To's

The willing years require parents to provide protection, action, and presence. Putting precious breakables out of reach works better than continually admonishing, "No, no! Don't touch." This little explorer is naturally drawn to anything shiny, colorful, breakable, and expensive! Because the drive to "know" an object by testing it with every sense organ is so much stronger than the capacity to remember that it is breakable, Mommy's, or not a toy, we save ourselves much energy and possible grief by putting the treasure away for now and "child-proofing" the house.

Taking a toddler to do something, like brushing teeth, is much more effective than *telling* him to do it. Our actions are more easily understood than our words. Singing a teeth-brushing song, taking our three-year-old by the hand, walking him to the bathroom, setting him on our laps, putting toothpaste on both ours and his brush, and brushing together appeals to his physically-focused capacities. Telling him to go brush his teeth from our easy chair falls into a vacuum he is intellectually and emotionally too young to fill. Telling him to do something over and over only creates frustration in us and teaches him to close his ears to our confusing, overwhelming demands.

A child in the willing years is an eager member of the family, wanting to be a part of everything. Our children learn best by imitating our actions, and really this is the only way they do learn at these ages. They learn by absorbing and imitating the activities around them, rather than by using the adult abilities of study and reflection. We must keep in mind that the focus of helping us sweep the floor is not, to our child, a clean floor. It is the *act of sweeping* in our presence that is so fulfilling. Our children benefit greatly from being encouraged to participate in simple household chores, but our expectations of the results must match their developmental stages. Sweeping the kitchen floor is our work, but it is their play and an extremely important part of their learning to be active family members.

> *When our family divided up chores, we wanted four-year-old Osmond to have a part, too. He chose picking up his toys, and we all thought that was great. When it came time for us to do our chores, the older kids finished theirs in record time. Poor Osmond sat in the middle of his room, surrounded by blocks and trains, in tears. The task was too big, and he hated being alone. When I said I would help drive his trains to the station, he was all smiles and an eager helper. I learned an important lesson. I have to be a good judge of what each of our children is able to do successfully. Otherwise, the task will be humiliating and defeating.*
>
> —*Larry, thirty-nine, father of three*

Gender Needs and Differences

Developmental growth varies between boys and girls and between siblings. What our first child accomplished at age six may not be perfected by our second one until age eight. Our sons may lag way behind our daughters in complexity of sentence structure, and our sons may develop upper body strength much earlier than our daughters. Rate of physical, emotional, and intellectual maturation are individual and unique for each child. We can expect, however, some gender variations in the themes of needs and development.

Between birth and seven girls and boys are more similar in development than at any other age. They both gain basic mastery over their bodies and explore their environments. We may, however, notice from the beginning that our son is more physical, much louder, and seems to take up more space, while our daughter is more verbal about things. One mother we know summed it up so neatly, "When I want to know where my daughter is, she tells me. When I want to find my son, I hear him."

Boys and girls need affectionate attention—cuddling, rocking, and singing—in equal proportion. A wrong-headed cultural habit is to wait too long to comfort little boys and to jump in too soon to help little girls. By ignoring or prolonging the discomfort of boys, because they must learn to toughen up to be masculine, we teach them to ignore their own pain, lose contact with their feelings, and lack trust that others will help or care. By jumping in too quickly to assist girls, because we think they must be more fragile to be feminine, we teach them to lack confidence in their own abilities, to be dependent upon others for help, and to feel entitled to constant support. On the playground, a close observer sees many variations of the cultural parenting stereotypes. A little boy falls out of his swing, the mother picks him up, holds him a moment, then says, "Okay, you're not hurt. Go on and play." He had been hurt when he fell from the swing, but Mommy says he isn't hurt, so confusion sets in. When this happens over and over again, the pain will no longer register at all. When a little girl struggles to get in or out of a swing, we see an almost automatic response to help her. How would she feel about herself had she struggled a little longer and succeeded in doing it on her own?

Give'ntake

During the willing years, our children appear to take more than they give. Because their focus of development is in the physical realm, they really have little ability to understand the principles of Family-Mind. Their awareness of the needs of others is limited by their own, huge needs. The FamilyMind Question, "What does this family need now, including me?" appears as a statement in the minds of toddlers, "I need; I need; I need." Their narcissistic perspective seems very one-sided.

If we observe carefully, however, we realize that they do give of themselves, and it falls to us to be open receptors. When we recognize that their giving is limited or enhanced by their developmental abilities, we are more attuned to and nurtured by what and how they give to us. Babies are wonderful givers. They give us their full attention when we look them closely in the eyes and talk to them; they reward us with a smile when we smile; they wildly kick their legs and stretch their arms to show us how glad they are to see us; they blossom under our care, striving to please us with each new accomplishment. Toddlers fill us up with their unrelenting admiration and wish to help us with anything and everything. They honor us by thinking we know all the answers; they include us in their play; and they trust us with their fears and joys, their tantrums and their successes.

Babies and young children are like sponges, absorbing the expressed and unexpressed emotions in their homes. The spiritual journey they set us on may be the greatest treasure any of us ever receive.

How To Make It Easier

Parents must be in charge during these early years. It is up to us to decide what our little ones need versus what they want. When our five-year-old sobs that he neeeeeeeeds the Power Ranger suit he saw on television, we have to ask ourselves, "Is this something that will nourish his imagination, enrich his play, and provide a positive role model? How will it affect him? How will it affect the family? How do we feel about it?" Of course, we consider his preferences, but the final decision is up to us. This responsibility is not so easily shouldered by those of us who were raised with the freedom of the "Me" generation. "But he wants it so badly," our hearts say, and we wonder what negative effects he will experience if his wants are denied. Be assured that if his needs for love, care, and safety are met, he will learn to value what he does have, and his grief over what he doesn't will soon fade.

Making the willing years easier on everyone also involves the creation of family routines, rhythms, and rituals. Children feel safe when they know what comes next. Being awakened in the same way each day, perhaps with a "Good morning!" song, eases the transition from sleep to wakefulness. Having a regular bedtime ritual, such as lighting a candle and saying a "Good night" prayer, reassures a child as she lets go of the day and drifts into sleep.

One of the most common ways we make the willing years harder is to offer our little ones too many choices. Too many things to choose from is confusing, and our children learn to expect to have a choice about everything. Just getting dressed can involve as many as twenty choices. "Do you want the red socks or the blue ones? A dress or jeans? Which hair ribbon do you want? The pink shirt or the printed turtleneck?" On and on we go, everyone becoming more frazzled and frustrated with each question. A child in the willing years responds best to few words, minimal choices, and brief or no explanations. Stating kindly but firmly, "*This* is the way we do things," as we do whatever it is with them, provides our children the boundaries that keep them safe and let them know what the family rules and expectations are. So many studies of families illustrate that children whose parents use benevolent leadership, expect family participation in proportion to developmental abilities, enforce firm limits, and follow through on the consequences, become respectful, creative, and contributing members of their homes and communities.[4]

The Feeling Years

The years of our children's lives from eight to twelve hold great challenges and require the development of inner resources to meet them. We may find, however, that we are at the mercy of an emotional pendulum that seems to swing with a hidden, uneven rhythm of its own. Sometimes we marvel at how well our nine-year-old takes care of himself, and then we see the same child at age twelve and wonder where his self-reliance went. The family must widen the circle of care around the child to allow for a new independence, while at the same time, preserving a safe place to return to when life gets rough and he feels small again. Our surveillance loosens as our children venture from the home into the outer world, following an inner drive to know how things work and why. The code words for parents during the feeling years are *steadiness*, *encouragement*, and *empathy*.

Focus of Development

During the willing years, the activities of feeling and thinking were on the back burner, and the will and body were the focus of development. When our son was angry, we saw it all over his body; his face scrunched up and got red, he balled his fists, and he stomped his feet. He had anger written all over him, but his feelings came and went quickly. Our eight- to twelve-year-old becomes much more sophisticated in the expression of feelings. His emotions last longer, and they are more complex. Our daughter begins to learn to delay gratification of her feelings: she can wait until tomorrow to go get ice cream, although she really wants to go today, or her embarrassment at being caught talking in class can await expression until she gets home to have a fit of tears or a temper tantrum. The expression of feelings shifts from being felt and seen all over the body to a more subtle communication. A heavy silence, a dark look, or a certain set of the jaw alerts us that feelings lurk just beneath the surface of her calm.

With the focus of development on the feeling life, our preteens waver between melancholy and euphoria; confident that the world is theirs, yet uncertain as to what this world is all about. Their expressions are sometimes raw, out of control, and bigger than they are. Easily angered, they rage about injustices, mistakes, and fears they have that we may not fully understand. Because intellectual development is on the back burner, their feelings may not make much sense to us, and our best approach is with compassion.

> *When my eleven-year-old son pushed his finger through*
> *the cellophane wrapper on a package of hamburger at*

*the market, I turned to him in astonishment and asked,
"Why did you do that?" He had the look of his four-
year-old self when he shrugged his shoulders and said,
"Gee, Mom, I just don't know." He looked so small and
confused that I just hugged him.*

—Marty, forty-five

These heart-filled emotions come most strongly during what Rudolf
Steiner, creator of Waldorf education, called the nine-year change.[5]
The passing of the fantasy life of childhood occurs during this
period, and children begin to sense that some things are not quite
what they appeared to be. With the realization that it was Mom and
Dad all along playing Santa Claus, for example, comes the dawning
of betrayal, sadness, and anger that life has to change so much. The
big chair in the living room that used to be a Queen's throne, a
pirate's frigate, or a rocket ship is no longer so malleable to their
imaginations. The old chair is just a chair, and they may sit in it
crosswise, their legs dangling over the side in frustration.

Family life may be disrupted by the developing fears of the child
living through the feeling years. This is the time for headaches, tummy
aches, nightmares, and upheavals in friendships. The ten-year-old will
begin to understand death for the first time, and the calling forth of
new strengths, skills, and abilities he did not know he had is cause for
fear and uncertainty. Although our daughter or son in the feeling years
has come down to earth, so to speak, and is in touch with the realities
of daily life, he or she often loses groundedness. Holding on to family
rules and boundaries provides our adventurous youngsters with a safe,
consistent place to express themselves.

How To's and How Not To's

Logical thinking and cognitive thought are still lingering on the
back burner of development, so our children in the feeling years still
respond best with simple choices and clear, uncomplicated directions. We can solicit their cooperation in family matters by appealing to their sense of belonging, fairness, and loyalty. For example, a
little boy we know wanted a set of airplane models for his birthday,

and because his buddy got them all, he thought he should get them all, too. His mother explained, "That is the way James' family has birthdays. Our family celebrates birthdays by giving one toy, one handmade gift, and one activity, such as one model airplane, a pencil holder, and a trip to the science museum." Being part of and carrying on family traditions, *his* family traditions, appealed to the boy, and later he remarked how his birthday seemed very full with a new model airplane, a pair of stilts, and a family trip to explore a local cave.

Making the family rules and customs clear give our preteens boundaries both to push against *and* feel safe within. Their growing independence does require a certain flexibility, and parents may feel confused about how strictly or how loosely to apply these limits. Our ten-year-old wants more control of how his life is organized, how his hair looks, what clothes he wears, how his room is decorated and arranged, and his chore schedule. These are all reasonable areas for children in the feeling years to apply their growing preferences, to test their likes and dislikes. And we parents have to choose our battles. It may be more important to deal with our daughter's refusal to do math homework, than to fuss that she wants to wear the color white all the time. Is it more crucial that our son play soccer or take viola lessons?

The decisions and dilemmas of the feeling years begin to test our culturally ingrained beliefs about what our children should be and should not be doing. Because friends begin to be an important part of our children's lives, their outside influences exert pressures to do and be like everyone else. The FamilyMind Question is helpful to keep us aware of what our children need in relation to our family's beliefs, customs, and needs, no matter what neighbors, friends, and extended family members believe and do.

The pressure from friends to watch TV really bothered our eleven-year-old, because we had sold ours long ago when he was six. We all sat down as a family and talked about what having a TV again would mean for us. After looking at what we do instead of watching TV, Harris declared that he didn't see how we would have the time. When his friends and their families watch TV, we make music, tell stories, solve mysteries, do crafts projects, garden, and tend to our animals. I was grateful that Harris still felt that family activities were so important.

—Pam, forty

Gender Needs and Differences

These are very active years for families when both boys and girls become interested in the world outside the home. Participation in sports, memberships in clubs, and lessons for all sorts of new interests bloom during these times. Boys, particularly, want to do everything with their fathers or other significant males, and it is especially important that men take active roles at this point in their boys' lives. Boys want to, literally, soak up the essence of their fathers or other respected males. A young man helping out in a third grade classroom is physically mobbed by the boys craving contact. Hanging on his back, arms, and legs, the man and the boys tussle, laugh, and tease each other. Fathers are begged to take their sons wherever they go, and fathers can often get cooperation from boys this age when mothers may have difficulty.

Mothers often feel a special sadness when being left out and may sense the passing of her son's childhood with some regret. The boy between eight and twelve does *not* have to cut his mother out of his life. His growth hinges on the transformation of their relationship from guide and protector to guide and cheerleader. Giving encouragement by being his biggest fan allows a mother to give her son what he most needs at this stage. A mother must allow a letting go to occur that releases her son to learn how to be a man, different from, yet still connected to, his mother. Her empathy and understanding of his struggle to become more himself lets a son know he can still come to her for comfort and advice.

Life for girls during the feeling years is often exciting, as they face little cultural restraint to be or act in certain, gender-defined ways. They are free to experiment and test their skills in the outside world. They will readily join a game of touch football with the boys without the hesitation or self-consciousness of the coming teen years. Encouragement and caution from fathers and empathy and reassurance from mothers provide girls with the courage to risk where they might otherwise be too timid or careful. Mastering skills that enhance self-confidence makes our daughters better prepared to enter the teen years when an alarming dip in self-esteem often occurs. Horseback riding, team sports, playing a musical instrument, dancing, planning a family vacation, starting a business, and so on, are all wonderful activities that challenge girls and reinforce a belief in themselves.

Give'ntake

Although both girls and boys are searching outwardly during the feeling years, their loyalty and sense of refuge remain within the family circle. What they experience and hear in the outer world are measured against what their family does, how their family thinks, or how their family normally reacts. Their developing feelings enable them to be more sensitive to the needs of family members, especially when pointed out, and this age group can be helpful once they understand what is expected of them. On the other hand, their high emotionality make them volatile and easily upset, often testing the patience and kindness of other family members.

The physical demands on parents change as our children grow older. The exhausting physical needs of babies and toddlers give way to the growing emotional needs of preteens, and our physical skills as chauffeur, audience, and catcher, guard, or goalie take front and center. We may have to stress the point of taking a bath, but once in the tub, our nine-year-old can accomplish this task on his own. Although self-reliance makes daily life easier for parents, we are not saying that getting a child in the feeling years to participate in family chores is easy. Like Tom Sawyer, our children can be very good at procrastinating, ignoring our requests, or talking someone else into doing it.

In the time it took for my brother to try to talk his way out of doing a chore, he could have had it done.

—Belle, fifty

The FamilyMind Question is still not thoroughly understood by our children from eight to twelve. They cannot step back and see the larger picture of family and individual needs. They can, however, observe and experience the reactions of others to their words and behaviors. Giving the appropriate feedback, such as "When you hit me, it hurts!" or "I feel bad when you call me stupid," begins the process of awakening children to the fact that they exist in relationship to others, not as center of the universe. During the feeling years, our children feel or sense needs more strongly than they can think about or meet them. We involve them by appealing to their strong sense of justice and fairness: by helping them make amends when they make mistakes; apologizing when they hurt others; choosing gifts that they know someone will like; and showing concern when a family member is ill. Speaking to the feeling content of the Family-Mind Question, such as saying "You're taking care of Grandma when you pick up your books," rather than the thinking content, such as "You must pick up your books, because Grandma can no longer see very well, and she might fall over them," works most successfully with our preteens.

How To Make It Easier

Learning not to take things too personally is a helpful parental survival skill that serves us well into the teenage years. The ups and downs of feelings may be difficult to bear at times, and it is important not to make our preteens older or more mature than they are. They are still young and thrive best with our genuine involvement and interest in their lives. As during the willing years, they still need clear limits and boundaries, a regular rhythm and routine, enough hours of sleep, plenty of affection, and firm, loving family support.

Children between eight and twelve flourish when they are involved in family projects, sports, clubs, birthday parties, sleep-overs, and schoolwork. They love the challenge of learning something new. Their abundant energy and enthusiasm needs careful nurturing and periods of alternation between activity and rest. Amidst all the action we can help our children renew themselves by encouraging them to read, play a musical instrument, sketch, lie in the grass looking at the clouds, care for a pet, garden, and take part in quiet family conversations. Activities for both the body and the soul will enhance their development into whole, feeling individuals.

The Thinking Years

When children become teenagers, they often feel they are on the outside of everything—their families, their peer groups, their culture, their world. Sometimes we wonder whether they have been exchanged with beings from another planet! The teen years are frequently tumultuous, because the psychological tasks of this time involve the development of intellectual and critical thinking, the evolution of a distinct self, and the search for the meaning of life. A large part of the teenager's struggle is to find just where he or she *does* belong. They may act out these confusing and uncomfortable feelings in a myriad of ways—by becoming super-competent in everything they do, by running away from home, by withdrawing from friends or activities they used to love, by breaking family rules, by becoming overly helpful or pleasing, by skipping school, by refusing to function as a committed member of the group, and so on. Their feelings of being outsiders often lead them to act as though they do not actually want to be part of the group. The message beneath their actions, however, states loudly and clearly, "I want to be loved. I want to belong, but I don't know if I can trust this family enough to show who I really am." Code words for these years are *nonattachment, nonjudgmental,* and *fair-but-firm.*

Focus of Development

The journey from childhood to individuation—the definition of a self—is sometimes treacherous for both parents and teens. Evolving from the symbiosis of infancy to the apart-ness of adolescence seems to happen in a flash. We look at our son's scratchy face and wonder where the baby soft skin went so soon. Between thirteen and eighteen teens develop the ability to think for themselves. They acquire their own ideas, search for answers to their own problems, and find a meaning in life that matches their own experiences. They

literally try on new ways of thinking and behaving from Socrates to
Marx, from introvert to extrovert.

> *From one week to the next, I'm never sure who I'm
> having breakfast with. One morning I got a lecture about
> how bad eating beef was, because the industry is
> destroying the rainforests. Then Dustin is asking me out
> for a hamburger. He's teaching me alot about not taking
> things for granted or pigeonholing people. The minute I
> make assumptions, I'm in trouble.*
>
> —*Mitch, forty-four*

They look at us with new, critical eyes, noting every discrepancy,
contradiction, and mistake we make. Nothing goes unexamined or
unquestioned. They stand on the outside and look in. They use us
as a sounding board in the best of circumstances and a carving
block in the worst-case scenarios. When we listen with a nonjudgmental attitude, they bring us their theories to discuss and expand
upon. One little hint that we consider their ideas outlandish,
unfounded, or immature, and they cut us up into little pieces and
spit us out—right back into our own faces. There is nothing so
scathing as an adolescent's critique of our behaviors. They cut to
the bone every time.

Another behavior we can expect from our teens is for them to push
the limits and boundaries we set. This testing is crucial for learning
where they begin and end, what the world will tolerate from them, and
the consequences of their behaviors upon themselves and others. We
parents serve as mirrors for our teens, reflecting back to them the
family rules, how their actions affect us, and what we expect of them.

How To's and How Not To's

This sometimes painful time for families is more bearable when
other family members hold fast to the belief that no matter what
behavior or theory a teen tries on she is still a member of the family
group, albeit a rather unpredictable one at the moment. Although we
may not condone what she says or does or how she looks, the

teenager needs our unwavering assurance that she belongs, that she will find her way, that the family group is supporting her in her search for self. Of course, we do not mean that "anything goes." Teenagers need firm limits and boundaries, fair consequences, and sensitive feedback about how their words and actions affect others.

Parents must continue to be leaders during the adolescent years. We are in charge of deciding upon curfews, acceptable activities, appropriate school performance, and our teen's role within the family. Family life is not a democracy. Our teens will be able to vote when they turn eighteen, but for now we know best and must have the last say. We are *not* suggesting that teens be treated as though they are living in a military academy. We must be firm but kind and consider their preferences. That our sixteen-year-old daughter longs for a slinky, black dress for the prom will be foremost in our considerations when we help her choose a dress. That she also wants a long, black limousine for herself and her friends may go against the safe boundaries we have set for her. She may have to make do with being driven in Dad's short, black four-door.

The limits and boundaries that keep our teens safe should be flexible and appropriate to our children. What is good for one teen may not work at all for another, and what worked in early adolescence may no longer meet the needs of our seventeen-year-old. We must also remember that what was right for us when we grew up may no longer fit the needs of our teens growing up in the world as it is now.

Calling a boy on the telephone for any reason was forbidden when I was a girl. A great deal of my daughter's social life happens on the phone talking with both boys and girls. They do homework, discuss date plans, work out disagreements, plot what to do about a troublesome friend, and generate creative ideas. We have to limit her time on the phone, so that other family members can use it, but the telephone is an important communication tool for her. Half of her connections would be gone if we forbid her to call boys.

—Marianne, fifty

With fair and safe boundaries go fair and appropriate consequences when our teens push the limits. It is vital that "the punishment fit the crime." We do not set an 9:00 P.M. curfew on weeknights to be mean. When our fifteen-year-old comes home after curfew, loses sleep, fails to get his homework done on time, and suffers the consequences with a poor grade or after-school study hall, he may begin to recognize weeknight curfews as practical rather than merely controlling. Grounding, a favored method for disciplining teenagers, may be overrated. It is true that by grounding our daughter, we can keep an eye on her, but how well does our taking away all of her privileges help her to understand *why* she should not do what she did? There are many teens who grimly suffer one grounding after another, never seeming to get the message their parents are trying to convey. Choosing a consequence that hits on a deeper level is more effective for teaching our children the inner boundaries they need when they are out in the world on their own. Here are some examples:

Broken Boundary	Consequences
late for curfew	curfew is set for 1 hour earlier
caught shoplifting	returns goods, apologizes to owner, and works off value in odd jobs; repeat performance secures a visit to juvenile hall to see what it is like
skips school	has to be accompanied to classes by a family member for 1 week
lies about whereabouts	must leave a detailed agenda of activities and phone home every hour for 1 week
caught smoking/drinking/doing drugs	need to know facts, so extensive research is required, including an interview with someone with emphysema, any illness or conditions related to alcoholism, or suffering the effects of drug addiction

failing to follow through on chores	if someone else had to do the chore, then both the required chore and the other person's chore will be completed next time they must be done
saying something cruel; showing disrespect	the person who is hurt tells how she/he feels, and a good deed is done for them

It is true that we must prepare our teenagers for adult life, but the real issue is, "What do we all need *now*?" The rules we set are based on family needs. The consequences are set to support those needs. Our suggested consequences will have meaning for some teens and others will not be fazed. Some children simply need to be reminded of rules and responsibilities, while others have to be knocked over the head with them. We parents must remember that, above all else, our own actions speak louder than any consequence we might give.

Gender Needs and Differences

Biology has a tremendous influence on the behavior of our sons and daughters during the thinking years. Parents may be astounded, and boys may be embarrassed, by any number of normal physical changes that occur: feet grow; voices wobble; facial, chest, and pubic hair become noticeable; body odor develops; erections occur regularly, often at inopportune moments; feet smell; and pimples erupt. The surge of testosterone drives boys to challenge themselves by pushing, sometimes quite literally, out into the world: they want the car; they want to hang out with their buddies; they take physical risks; they achieve at sports. Some boys stay put physically but challenge themselves mentally with endless hours on the computer or with video games. Others act out by challenging their teachers, parents, or other authority figures. And all boys this age are gripped by the fantasy and reality of sex. Boys have a hard time participating in family life when they are being pushed and pulled in so many different directions.

*I was amused one night when my fourteen-year-old said, "Mom, I'm going over to Patrick's house tonight." I said, "Aren't you forgetting an important step here? Mom, **may** I go over to Patrick's house tonight?"*

—Wilma, forty-three

A girl's biology, while also hormonally charged, often manifests differently. The changes in her body, such as the accumulation of fat on the hips, thighs, breasts, and buttocks, a sudden growth spurt in height, or the appearance of acne, may make her self-conscious, self-critical, and more susceptible to depression. What we may interpret as self-indulgent moodiness may, in fact, be a serious struggle with self-discovery. This normal turning inward is complicated by the teenage milieu of increased social activities and academic expectations, leaving little time for calm self-reflection or family participation.

My daughter seemed to love the flurry of ballgames, parties, school projects, and club officers' responsibilities when she was sixteen. Looking back now I realize that she would go full steam ahead for a few weeks, and then she would crash at home with a bad cold, stomach ache, bad cramps, or depression. She'd sleep all day at those times. Now I wonder whether she'd have been better off with fewer activities and more chance to stay rested along the way.

—Sylvia, fifty-five

Give'ntake

During the middle of the thinking years, our teens become capable of considering a situation or person from another's perspective. The FamilyMind Question, "What does this family need now, including me?" takes on new meaning as young people intellectually puzzle out the dilemma. Their thinking may be immature and unformed at times, but the fact that they are considering their own needs *with* the needs of others is the real achievement.

Skill development for both boys and girls is important during the teen years, and the family is a logical arena for practice. Learning to cook and being responsible for one family dinner per week is a great opportunity to tune to others' needs in terms of food preferences, schedules, and so on. As our children grow older, they grow into bigger roles within the family and can contribute more on the give'ntake scale. Rather than setting the table, for example, they can now be responsible for meal planning, making shopping lists, meal preparation, or cleanup. They can help younger siblings with homework or hobbies. To avoid being a sullen lump in the back seat on family vacations, teens can take an active role in planning the itinerary, calculating mileage, or mapping out the route. Teens can lead family prayers, organize an outing, and plan holiday activities. The point is to keep our teenage children as actively involved in family life as possible.

The difficulty here is that a daughter or son may be physically at home but not mentally present enough to participate. Shut up in their rooms with a set of headphones permanently attached, they create their own culture of music, language, dress, art, and recreation that leave us totally on the outside and usually baffled. Opening the door to a teenager's room can be like stepping on the surface of another planet. Why do they like it so dark? How can they stand that loud, discordant "music"? What do they do in there for hours and hours?

Because they do not believe that we understand them, we are a constant embarrassment to them, and our teens often choose the company of their friends over family activities. When they push us away, we may be tempted to take them at their words and leave them to fill their own time, to live their own lives. They certainly seem, at times anyway, to be able to take care of themselves. The circle of care around our maturing children does indeed need to expand. However, it is a mistake to leave the door open too long; our teens need a closed door to butt their heads against, because that same door keeps out the world, providing a safe refuge when life becomes too demanding, too confusing, or too risky. Insisting they take part in family matters may be greeted with mumbles and grumbles, sullen silences, or nasty outbursts. Giving reasons for their participation, such as, "You'll thank us for this when you're older," or "Being part of our family now will help you when you have your own family," simply increases their resistance. A simple, "This is how *our* family does things," is enough.

How To Make It Easier

We cannot stress enough that when dealing with teens, we must pick our battles carefully. When every movement our teens make comes under parental scrutiny, they get the message that we do not trust them. Concentrate on things that have real impact on family members and learn to let the little, annoying things go. Apply the Family-Mind Question, "What does this family need now, including me?" when weighing the importance of a haircut, a tattoo, the car keys, or a curfew.

> *My dad constantly hounded me about the music I liked, how I wore my hair, the kind of pants I wore, and whether I made my bed in the mornings. I grew up thinking that there was nothing about me that my dad liked or approved of.*
>
> *—Rick, thirty-four*

Another way to live more comfortably with our teens *is to learn to not take their words or actions personally.* Careless actions or thoughtless words can hurt, and we may find ourselves wondering what we did wrong or where we failed in our parenting. The truth is that our children are testing the world, and are often unsure or unaware of the consequences. They say and do things with an awkwardness that often gets them into trouble. *Looking for the positive intent beneath words and actions gets us to the real matter.* When our daughter rolls her eyes and sarcastically says that we do not understand anything at all about her or her life, we could interpret her words like this: "You don't listen to me. I feel judged by your criticisms. I desperately want you to know me for who I am and not your idea of who you want me to be." When our son skips classes, his behavior suggests a number of problems: "I don't feel I belong here. Something is wrong at school. I feel overwhelmed and need a break. I've been trying to tell you something but you wouldn't listen, so I'll do something you will take notice of." And so on. Getting to the deeper meaning of words and actions may still not make much sense to us, but our children will feel our support and care. Knowing that we do not understand but are willing to listen without blame or judgment reassures our teens that they are important, that we value their opinions, feelings, and ideas. Lectures and criticism close off any possibility for an alliance, invite misunderstanding, and inspire anger and rebellion. Taking a "tell me more about that" position opens the way for connection, support, and a sense of belonging. And no matter how their actions convince us to the contrary, our children truly *want* to belong in their families.

The Young Adult Years

When our children leave home to go to college, to go to work, to get married, to travel around the world, to find their own lives, a shift in our expectations must occur. How much and how often they participate in family activities and how much weight their opinions carry depend upon the other commitments they make in their lives, how far away they are from home, and their financial situations.

> *We have five children, and my hardest time after all left home was the first Thanksgiving. Ted was in France, Margie was committed to her first job in Texas, Al was in the military, James had made ski plans with friends, and Robbie was away across the country in college. The house felt huge, cold, silent, sad, and lonely without them. Frank and I decided to fly to Hawaii to spend Thanksgiving on the beach.*
>
> *—Catherine, fifty-six*

When young adult children come home after college, the military, a divorce, or for whatever reason, family rules must be reviewed and renegotiated. What worked for a teenager will no longer be appropriate for a twenty-three-year-old. Our older children are now able to give and receive in proportion to what is needed by the whole family. Children who have been out on their own should take a more responsible role in making the family work. They can be expected to pay rent, contribute to food costs, do grocery shopping, do their own laundry, do some household cleaning—especially their rooms and bathrooms—and cook several nights a week. They should alert whomever is in charge that they have used the last of the laundry detergent, drank the last beer, and used the last vacuum cleaner bag, or replace the items themselves. If the grown children accept their share of family responsibilities, they deserve the respect and freedom of adult members of the family. All of the details of family life will have to be renegotiated according to the FamilyMind Question, "What does everyone need now, including me?" We sympathize with the mother who asked us the following question on-line in *ParentSoup*: [6]

Q: I am feeling very distressed and frustrated with my son who will be 21 in December. I am just not sure how to feel or handle this situation. He and a friend shared an apartment and he decided he'd had enough of the city and moved. Not quite correct…left. His roommate friend also didn't want to live there anymore and moved back in with his mother. My son left many things and has more or less left it up to me to clean up his mess and take care of things. He left a kitten and many articles of furniture and personal belongings. He left my phone number for people to contact regarding his things. I have a daughter that is due to have a baby any day now. I don't have time to keep running over to his place. Now the complex is calling me wanting to know what to do about his apartment and wanting it cleaned out. How should I feel and handle this? Part of me wants to tell my son I don't ever want to see him again for what he has done and I will go over and take care of it.

A: You ask how you SHOULD feel. How DO you feel? In your position we would feel pretty upset, angry, and disappointed in our son's irresponsible and thoughtless behavior. It's time for Mom to stop coming in and picking up the pieces of his life! First, find the kitten a home. You really cannot get around that one. Whose name is the apartment in? If it is not in your name, tell the apartment folks that you are not responsible for the stuff left or the cleaning. Tell them that leaving your number was a mistake, and give them your son's number. Tell your son that you will not be helping him with the apartment. You do not need to give reasons, excuses, or apologies. This is his to deal with. If the apartment is in your name, then you have some decisions to make. One solution is to have the stuff hauled off to the dump or thrift store and have the apartment cleaned. Send the bill for it all to your son. We doubt you will see your money back, but we would make it all very professional by sending the expenses in bill form with scheduled payments, when they start, how much they are, when you expect it to be paid off, your signature, and a place for his. Request that he send you back a signed and dated copy. The other alternative is, of course, for you to bend over backwards to clean out the apartment and feel resentful toward your son. Hopefully, you can forgive him later. Our kids must learn to be responsible for their actions, and now is a perfect time for your son to begin. Best wishes!

Living on Planet Parenthood

In the past, children were taught the commonly accepted moral, social, and religious values, and that was that. No questions asked; no shades of gray. Today, however, parents are challenged in ways our grandparents never dreamed of. Not only must we adjust to the dramatic changes children bring to our lives, we must also deal with the evolution of the family itself caused by our rapidly changing culture. Whether we are a two-parent, heterosexual-couple family, a gay-couple family, a single-parent family, a step-parent family, an adopted-child family, a foster family, an intergenerational family, a chosen and gathered-together family, we all face the same obstacles and grapple with the same dilemmas. All parents wrestle with the complexities of helping our children deal with the pressures of doing drugs, of having sexual relationships, of buying into materialism, and of having to look and act a certain way to be accepted and popular. How do we create an environment that will keep our children safe yet still be stimulating enough for them? How do we keep them involved in the family while giving them the freedom to explore the world beyond it?

Our children, from birth to seven, are totally dependent upon us for their care and live at the far end of the give'ntake model in a state of overreceiving. This is perfectly normal and natural, because, until they are older, they have no concept of what others need. From eight to twelve, our children become loyal family members, able to take a more active part in daily family chores, decisions, and nurturing activities. They have a growing—albeit momentary—sense of what others need. From thirteen to eighteen, our teens waver between the outer culture of their peers and the inner sanctuary of the family. We may have to insist on the degree of family participation of which they are now capable, but they are able to show respect, concern, and care for other family members, as well as for themselves. And finally, our young adult children are an important source of support and enrichment to the family circle, as they come and go in our lives, bringing their experiences, opinions, and questions from the outside world.

This planet of parenthood holds extraordinary treasures and adventures we never before imagined. We are called upon to be "on duty" twenty-four hours a day, and are pushed to discover and cultivate strengths and resources we did not know we possessed. We learn to see the world again through a beginner's eyes.

> *I am constantly amazed at the delight my baby takes in the world. I had forgotten how entertaining a ceiling fan can be!*
>
> —*Sharon, twenty-nine*

We are forced to ponder tough answers to hard questions. We are loved and admired unconditionally beyond anything we ever dreamed we would ever deserve.

> *My nine-year-old was relentless in wanting to know where I was going, what was I going to do, could he go too, could he help me work? What if, somehow, my behavior failed to live up to his expectations of me? What if I could not answer his important questions? I lived in awe of his devotion.*
>
> —*Henrí, forty*

We must cross-examine every value, every moral belief, and every political position we've ever held. We become accountable for every action and are held responsible for every outcome we had heretofore given little thought to.

> *With two teenagers, family meals have become cross-examinations and frantic pleas to the jury to consider our position.*
>
> *—Sienna, forty-five*

Whether we realize it or not, and few of us do in the beginning, when we become parents, we embark upon a spiritual journey that will lead us into the darkest and deepest valleys and up to the highest, most glorious summits we can possibly imagine.

> *I have many roles: husband, musician, therapist, friend.*
> *My favorite name is "Dad."* [7]
>
> —Bruce Silverman, Founder and Leader,
> *The Sons and Daughters of Orpheus*

Endnotes: Part Ten

1. Maggie Scarf, *Intimate Worlds: Life Inside the Family* (New York: Random House, 1995), xxxv.

2. Gilbert Childs, *Steiner Education in Theory and Practice* (Edinburgh, UK: Floris Books, 1991), 40-43.

3. Anne Lamott, *Operating Instructions: A Journal of My Son's First Year* (New York: Pantheon Books, 1993), 154.

4. Lawrence Steinberg, *Beyond the Classroom* (New York: Simon and Schuster, 1996).

5. Hermann Koepke, *Encountering the Self: Transformation and Destiny in the Ninth Year* (Hudson, NY: Anthroposophic Press, 1989).

6. Don Elium and Jeanne Elium, "Ask the Family Counselor," http://www.parentsoup.com, and on American Online, keyword ParentSoup.

7. Bruce Silverman, founder and director of *The Sons and Daughters of Orpheus*, in a conversation with the authors, Walnut Creek, CA, 22 July 1995.

PART ELEVEN

Men, Women, and FamilyMind— He Said/She Said

*If only we could all accept that there
is no difference between us
where human values are concerned.*

—Liv Ullman

❧ ❧ *DON* | Men have been culturally trained for thousands of years to be hunters and protectors. The call to action is in our genes, and whether it be in farming, office work, sports, or warfare, each of us embodies and shares a rich and meaningful heritage by virtue of our birth as males. These skills as provider and protector insured the survival of humankind and worked effectively in a variety of environments. As part of modern civilization, however, these same skills severely limit my participation in family life, cut me off from my own feelings, and take me places I may not really want to go.

❧ *JEANNE* | Women come from a long lineage of gatherers and nurturers, hearth-tenders and healers. For thousands of years, our ability to give birth, nurture and care for children, and our skills at nursing the sick, cooking, tending the fires, sewing, and home-building have also secured the survival of humankind. Since our emergence into the modern world, our skills have been devalued, trapping us in low-paying jobs and in unequal and unsatisfying relationships. I am stuck trying to nurture others in the context of a world gone mad over commercialism, materialism, and intellectualism.

> **DON** | Men have been biologically primed for the hunt. Our eyes are developed to focus on a single goal—making the kill, scoring the goal, closing the deal. Our bodies are fueled by testosterone, giving us physical strength, a continuous tension buildup/release cycle, the urge to take risks—the bigger the better—tougher skin, and an instinct for action over communication.

> **JEANNE** | With more rods and cones at the sides of our eyes[1] women developed a wider peripheral vision for keeping watch over the children. We are skilled at seeing the bigger picture and noting details—"Ellen wore a yellow, empire-waist dress with matching shoes; Jill was dressed in pink silk; and Harriet wore green wool." We seem to be more physically sensitive all over our bodies and intuitively sensitive to the needs and feelings of those around us. Estrogen and progesterone urge us toward including, understanding, and supporting others.

> **DON** | Men have been trained to put everything aside that does not in some way directly relate to or assist in the pursuit of the goal. Personal needs go on the back burner. Our children have to wait for our attention and affection. Friendships are neglected. Community crises stand in line. Environmental issues have to be considered tomorrow. Everything but the goal must be put off at all costs. When I concentrate exclusively on a goal, I lose touch with what is also meaningful in my life: my dreams, my feelings, my deeper purpose—I feel cut off and lonely.

> **JEANNE** | Because the needs of others and society's expectations are so great, women are taught to ignore or deny their own needs, wants, and wishes. We become stuck in serving, enabling,

and empowering others at the expense of our own development. When I see only the needs of others, I lose touch with my own ideas, opinions, goals, needs, dreams, power, and self-hood.

⟨⟩ ⟨⟩ Don | The changes brought about by the technological age have left us confused about traditional male roles as hunters and providers. Pursuing a career is no longer a male privilege that our culture, our neighborhoods, and our families support and protect. Unlike the hunters of old, when we return home we are expected to help with the kids and take an active part in household chores. We often feel inept at home in the world of feelings, because we are so out of touch with our own.

⟨⟩ Jeanne | A woman's "work" of creating a safe haven where families survive and thrive has been reduced to cleaning, washing, shopping, chauffeuring, and cooking. Today's economy and culture demand that we become both mothers and career women, spread so thin that we have become paragons of organization, efficiency, and time management. We feel guilty, because we know our children need more of our time and attention, yet we feel compelled to strive and succeed in our careers.

⟨⟩ ⟨⟩ Don | Most of us sense that we did not receive all we needed from our parents. Within us is a place that feels empty, silent, and cold. We harbor a deep desire to not let this happen with our own children, but we are afraid of losing our manhood in the process. We wonder, "Must we become more like women to be good fathers and husbands?"

⟨⟩ Jeanne | Because women have to be more efficient at home and at work, we have learned to think in terms of goals, schedules, and lists. We have been told that our sensitivity, our concern for the needs of others, and our interest in relationships are hindrances in the workplace. The habit of WorkMind thinking becomes so ingrained that we use it everywhere. Although we sense the loss of something vital and deeply alive as we become more masculine, we are not quite sure what it is we have lost.

⁂ ⁂ *DON* | Some awakening force within us is challenging our old, narrow roles. We long to do meaningful work that is of value to us, our families, and our communities. We want to feel love and belong in our families. Many of us want to get to know our children, our wives, our neighbors. When we come home, we want to really be there, in tune with our families, and our families tuned in with us.

⁂ *JEANNE* | We want to project a positive voice into the workplace and our communities without compromising our own needs or the needs of our mates and our children. We want to be valued for the life-sustaining, nurturing, and homemaking skills our families so desperately need. We want to be supported by our culture as working mothers at home with our children or mothers working outside of our homes, sustained with better-than-adequate child care, family health benefits, and educational opportunities.

⁂ ⁂ *DON* | The Women's Liberation Movement gave women more access to the external worlds of educational and career opportunities. The Men's Movement has been, in part, a Men's "Revelations" Movement. Our quest has been an internal one to discover "Who am I, really?" and "How do my hunting and protecting roles have to be broadened and redefined to promote life in these times?" and "How can I be actively involved both at work and at home?" and "What are my needs?" "What is important to me?" and "How do I really feel about important things?"

⁂ *JEANNE* | Women have been through so many relationships, so many hurts, and so many disappointments, I sometimes wonder whether we were meant to coexist with men at all. Perhaps there was value in the ancient Amazon culture, where women and men had their own camps and came together only to socialize and procreate.

DON   After co-writing our first two books, *Raising a Son* and *Raising a Daughter*, Jeanne and I knew that something was missing in the relationships between women and men and even more so in relationships within the family. Proud as I was of my male heritage and the good I could do, I feared that my male hard-wiring precluded home-minded thinking. I struggled to find my own style of fathering, rather than trying to emulate the mothering that Jeanne did. I feared that to be nurturing meant being a wimp. Could I still be a man *and* be an active, involved caring member of my family?

JEANNE   As Don became more actively involved at home, I worried about what he would actually do, whether he would do a good job, and if I would still have as important a role. Would I still have some power and some say about things at home? Or would this be another place where a man interfered and then took over?

DON   One of my male clients fearfully reported back to me after talking about FamilyMind with a golfing buddy: "My best friend told me that it sounded like I was giving in to whatever my wife wants; that she will take my manhood and squeeze all of the life out of it." "How is your buddy's personal life going?" I asked him. He paused, then laughed uneasily. "Well, now that I think about it, he has been divorced twice, has three kids he sees once a month, has a girlfriend half his age, and he probably has a drinking problem."

JEANNE   At a weekly session of a women's group, I was in tears. "My husband acts like a teenager," I sobbed. To my amazement, this group of empathetic and caring women burst into laughter. "What's so funny?" I wailed. "They all do," they told me.

DON | No matter how hard I fought it, I *felt* like a teenager at home. My hunting mode created the effect of a bull in a china closet or a passive-aggressive pouter. The harder I tried to be heroic, the more I missed the current needs of my family and lost touch with my own personal needs. Raising a family is like floating on a sea of ever-changing needs and priorities. When a man locks into the hunter mode at home, his behavior gets out of sinc with the flow of needs, and he looks like a selfish, self-centered, impulsive, teenager. This may not be his intention, but it is the effect.

JEANNE | I don't want to have to train a husband how to be at home. Why can't he open his eyes and look around? There is too much to do, and I am too exhausted to have to do it all alone AND teach another adult how to see to all our needs.

DON | Many of us are afraid to embrace the feeling life that is so familiar to women. What if we are devoured by it? What if we lose ourselves? What if we lose our masculinity? The foreignness of it scares us, because so few of us had fathers who were both firm and kind, could shed tears and still be strong. We have not been taught that the way of the reed carries the most strength, because it is able to bend and survive a windstorm, whereas the rigid tree will snap in two. I am learning and am trying to teach other men that FamilyMind requires the strength of the reed, firm yet flexible.

JEANNE | I hate to admit it, but many of us are so rigid about how things should be done at home that we allow no room for help or for the real needs of family members, or our own, to be considered. I try to get everything done by myself, because I believe that *I* have to do it, I'm the one who is *supposed* to do it, or I'm the only one who can do it *right*. I push my stubborn self beyond the limits of my energy where I lie broken in the wake of a storm of unmet needs.

    DON | From my own experiences and from those of other men I work with, FamilyMind is not an easy thing to learn. It is not a quick-fix technique. Nor does it require becoming like a woman. It requires opening to a new way of thinking. It means developing a new lifestyle. And the good news is that men *can* learn to think in FamilyMind. We are the early pioneers stumbling down a path that I once feared did not exist.

    JEANNE | FamilyMind thinking is not something that women are just naturally good at and men have to struggle to learn. Many women lose sight of family needs in the midst of getting laundry done, getting the house cleaned for a party, preparing for the influx of company on a crisp Thanksgiving day. We get locked into WorkMind thinking and later wonder why everything was so hard and so exhausting.

    DON | As I get better at changing my goal-focused thinking to personal, need-focused thinking at home, asking the FamilyMind Question becomes more natural. For example, my usual way of walking down the hall to my son's playroom was often a straight, step-over-whatever-is-in-the-way-goal-oriented stroll. One day, early on in my stumbling attempts to use FamilyMind, we were headed down the hall, and a laundry basket full of warm towels was just sitting there in front of the linen closet in the middle of our path. Before I learned to use FamilyMind, I would trip over the basket, not notice it, or be irritated that someone left it in the hallway. This time I found myself saying to my son, "Let's sit down and fold towels." I dumped them over his head, and we started folding and kidding around.

    JEANNE | When I discovered the two of them, I was confused. This was new behavior for my guys. What do I do? My first thought was, "Well, I'll just have to fold them over again when they're done playing around." Letting go of the expectation that things, like folding towels, have to be done just so continues to be a challenge for me. I always think of my friend Laura who says, "I don't care how the things are folded; just so they're put away out of sight!"

DON I cherish the memory of that event because I behaved differently. I found myself doing what needed to be done in as playful a way as possible. Like putting on a new pair of glasses, I now have a wider, clearer view, no longer focused on just one task at a time. Needs just jump out in front of me, and I find ways to meet them as best I can. If I make an effort to make meeting the need as enjoyable as I can, it is easier for my children to get involved.

JEANNE I grew up in a family that lived through the Great Depression. They learned to cherish and take pride in the possessions they had and to care for them religiously. Keeping a full linen closet with carefully starched, ironed, and folded sheets and towels was very satisfying to my granny. I loved to walk inside and run my fingers over the silky softness of the linen. And the smell, so deliciously sweet and fresh! Today I yearn for a linen closet like my granny's, but they don't make them like that anymore. Today, I'm happy about seeing my son's smiling face just before I bury him in a pile of fresh towels, warm from the dryer.

DON I used to feel like a stranger in my own house. I didn't know where most essential items were kept, not to mention those things we only used once in awhile. This hall scene is one of my "continuing revelations," and I reflect upon it often. When I feel tired, upset, and overwhelmed, asking myself, "What do we really need here?" gets me out of my pout and back into giving and receiving what is most important. Daily tasks are best dealt with as things that just need to be done, because they need to be done, not as prizes from the hunt or forces to defeat. No heroes, no prisoners, and no trophies, but maybe some fun and enjoyable memories of doing regular stuff together.

⊰ *JEANNE* | Today Don broke the sugar bowl; a sugar bowl an old friend brought me from England. How I mourn that sugar bowl, its delicate blue flowers on a white ground. I might have taken the accident as a personal attack: that he does not care about possessions that mean a lot to me; that I just do not deserve to have nice things; that his clumsiness was a deliberately careless act against me. Then I look at our situation closely. We are supporting each other to do what needs to be done. I'm here typing away on this book, and he is washing dishes after breakfast. Anyone could have dropped that lovely little sugar bowl, and Don promises that someday we'll go to England to get another one.

⊰ ⊰ *DON* | A best friend I have had the privilege of knowing for over ten years has always been supportive of my work and inspired an article I wrote called, "What a Man Needs That a Woman Can't Provide." When his romantic relationship matured into marriage, he became very interested in the concept of Family-Mind. He recently mentioned to me that it changed not only his home life but his "male circle at parties" conversations. "At parties, the guys always gravitate into one group and the women to another. One night a friend started the 'I hate the honey-do list' conversation. I was surprised to hear myself saying, 'You know, she isn't angry at you because you don't finish the list perfectly. She is really mad because she has to make the list in the first place; she has to do all the thinking about the needs of the family—what needs to be done, when, and with whom. When she hands you the list, she thinks, 'The least you can do is finish the list correctly.' What she really wants is for you to join in the *thinking* about what goes on the list.' The conversation got pretty stimulating at that point. Some guys got it, while other guys put me on their wimp list. I loved every minute of it. It's really not about gender. It's about applying your gender to the right way of seeing what family is all about. I am by no means a FamilyMind expert, but once I understood the differences between the needs of work and the needs of home, it all made sense. What a salvation for family relationships!"

JEANNE When we first started using FamilyMind in our family, the very worst thing Don could do was to act like an expert or to point out when I wasn't using it. I don't know why it was so infuriating to be instructed in something having to do with the family. I'm already supposed to know it all, right? If not then somehow I had failed at being a real woman. And I didn't want to get my hopes up that Don would start being a real partner with me at home.

DON When my male clients try on the new lens of FamilyMind thinking, they find themselves just naturally doing what needs to be done and noticing what they have never seen before. One client was still trying to be the hero instead of a member of his family. Thinking that he was helping out, he would start washing the car right when dinner was ready, or flip on the computer just before it was time to take his daughter to school. I explained FamilyMind and wrote the FamilyMind Question on a small card for him to carry with him. His homework assignment was to think of the question three times as he touched the door knob before entering his home, and then to repeat it to himself throughout the evening. Above all, I told him NOT to tell his wife what he was doing. With nothing else to try, and desperate to save his marriage, he agreed. To my surprise, he brought his wife to the next session. She explained, "I don't know what you are doing, but I want you to know I like the direction it's going. I'm confused and very suspicious, because this is what happened the other day. I got home from the grocery store, and he came out to help me carry in the groceries. This was a shock, because I can't remember the last time he helped with something like that. We haven't been doing so well together, so I was on my guard. Not only did he get the groceries in, but our young son hurt his finger in the midst of all this, and Jon told me that he would finish the groceries. Later I asked him, 'Where

are the eggs?' He said with a puzzled look, 'In the refrigera-
tor.' I asked, 'Why?' He said, 'Because they belong there.' He
ALWAYS leaves the eggs out on the counter. You really don't
understand how big a change this is. You might think I am
being silly, but I am on the verge of leaving him because I'm
so exhausted, and he is so distracted. To have him finish what
he started was a shock. I asked him what was going on, but he
wouldn't tell me. He said if I wanted to know, I should come
here with him, so here I am."

◁▷ *JEANNE*   Women sense the FamilyMind way of thinking and try to
explain it. Men listen, but hear it come out, "If you were a
woman, you'd understand." When we approach the problem
from a "goals vs. need" focus, both men and women understand. We need not get entangled in the gender question at
all. Both women and men can rally around the guiding FamilyMind Question. "What does this family need now, including me?" embodies what everyone needs. It is a big enough
question to include gender differences, but it does not make
us prisoners of our biology in the context of family communications.

◁▷ ◁▷ *DON*   During the "Don't tell anyone what you are doing yet" phase
of FamilyMind, one client reported that he tried practicing
the FamilyMind Question everywhere. He told us, "It's actually fun. I feel less hurried, more aware, and more in touch
with those around me. I had lunch at McDonalds one day,
and a small group of young kids were having a birthday party
there. The only seat left was beside them. Usually, I'd be so
over-focused on work that I'd just block them out. Since I
didn't have anything pressing, I just watched and listened to
the chaos. It was quite cute, and it was a mess. As the parents
were starting to clean up, I found myself saying to them,
'Why don't you go ahead, and I'll put the rest of the trays
away for you.' They looked so dazed and tired that I laughed.
I felt so much better when I returned to my office. The FamilyMind Question allows me to be more in tune with others

and what is really happening, both inside myself and outside, and I often feel recharged and refreshed after a goal-focused day at work."

JEANNE   The down side of the information age is that work is too accessible—no matter where we are we can check in by modem or cell phone. We can work twenty-four hours a day. This dedication to work may lead to material wealth but at what cost to family and personal needs? WorkMind and FamilyMind are part of an ever-revolving cycle that refreshes and regenerates us as long as we allow them to shift in our lives and not be stuck in one mode or the other.

DON   We received the following letter from a man in one of our audiences:

Dear Don and Jeanne,

Thank you so much for teaching us the idea of Family-Mind. It saved my marriage and gave me a new hope for living my life. However, please warn others that Family-Mind can quickly fade away if you do not stay aware. After a good year full of changes, I became extremely busy at my work, and I stopped using FamilyMind without realizing it. Things got tense again in my marriage, but using the FamilyMind Question made it easier to recover. I needed a good whack on the head to get back on track. We need something to remind us to keep on practicing. Maybe you should put a warning label on FamilyMind, "Warning: Will quickly perish unless practiced and lived just one day at a time."

Sincerely,
Bill Slater

JEANNE   So many women have confessed to me that their husbands focus on family needs better than they do. Yet, most of us expect women to lead the way in seeing to family needs, and women bear the blame when family needs are not met.

Because of our biology, psychology, and training, women are expected to be in charge of home and family, whether we have the skills or not. The discovery that we also have untapped powers and skills that the outside world desperately needs piles more expectations onto an already overloaded pair of shoulders: the Supermom, the stay-at-home mom, the career mom, the single mom, and the married mom. Where does "Me, Myself, and I" figure in? When am I a person, apart from being Mom? FamilyMind provides an opportunity to pioneer an extremely challenging frontier: caring for and being part of a family while INCLUDING ourselves.

❧ ❧ DON | I used to agree with other men that I just couldn't do housework and care for kids the same way, or even as well, as a woman could. We just weren't programmed for it. I didn't give it too much thought until it became an issue in my own life. I discovered that we can develop the nurturing and caring parts of ourselves that are deep within us, long dormant because our culture has not expected us to bring them to life.

❧ JEANNE | Whether we are good at it or not, we have been bred and trained to care for others, often at the expense of ourselves. Some women have not faired well under this pressure and collapse into physical or mental illness. Some have left marriages and children, unable to carry this burden and live their own lives. Our souls are hungry for our own identities. Today, when we ask the FamilyMind Question, we must pay special attention to the "including me" part. The FamilyMind Question is the only guide I have found that helps me get to the real needs—my own and those of my family.

❧ ❧ DON | Most men I meet do not know what they need. When I ask them, they stare into space or give me a blank look. "I'm not sure I know how to know," one client said with sadness. "My wife is always accusing me of taking care of my own needs and only mine; never paying much attention to the rest of the family. But, look, I work a forty-five hour week to make enough money for the house we have; I commute over an hour each way to work, so we can have the house we have. If I were doing this only for myself, I wouldn't be working forty-five hours a week or living in this house! I'd have a little apartment over a small country store, where I could go fishing whenever I had a mind to."

JEANNE   Most of us have difficulty knowing what we need, because we have been taught to focus on the needs of others. We've lost touch with or no longer recognize our own. Many of us learned that our needs were not really very important, and if the work got done and everyone else was cared for, then we could do something we liked as a reward. Trouble is, the work is never done, and everyone else's needs seem endless.

DON   A widowed mother I know was stunned when a counselor revealed that her nine-year-old son was worried about her and concerned that she didn't have any friends. This concern was causing him to have great anxiety and panic attacks at school. "After my husband died, Evan and I became very dependent upon each other. We formed a sort of cocoon around us to insulate us from the grief of our loss." Without really realizing it, she had cut herself off from friends to care for her son and to shield them both from feeling their pain. "When I began to see friends again and to spend some time alone, the grief came washing over me. If I didn't know that Evan needed me to get on with my own grieving and living my own life, I might have retreated back into that safe cocoon. Now he's free to do his own grieving, and we're both more alive."

JEANNE   We may think we are serving our families, but if we ignore or deny our own needs, we narrow the space for *others* to give and receive. By watching us do it, our children learn to be sensitive to their own needs and to care what others need. That is a gift that our world cannot do without.

Endnotes: Part Eleven

1. Anne Moir and David Jessel, *Brain Sex* (New York: Dell Publishing, 1989), 18.

PART TWELVE

The New Pioneers

Thus, when a certain critical number achieves an awareness, this new awareness may be communicated from mind to mind. Although the exact number may vary, the Hundredth Monkey Phenomenon means that when only a limited number of people know of a new way, it may remain the consciousness property of these people.

But there is a point at which if only one more person tunes-in to a new awareness, a field is strengthened so that this awareness reaches almost everyone!

...Your awareness is needed....You may be the "Hundredth Monkey"....[1]

—Ken Keyes, Jr.,
The Hundredth Monkey

Our culture is approaching critical mass: No matter our income level, our career choice, our family configuration, our race, our political affiliation, or our spiritual beliefs, women and men are being challenged to build a new structure for family life. The work of our times pits the needs of families and the individual against the ethics of Big Business in a Global Economy: Do or Die, Produce or Get Out, Perform No Matter the Cost. We are led to believe that we can do it all; we must simply learn to be more efficient. The results of our improved efficiency are predictable without exception—family members feel more and more like items to be checked off a list. "Yes, Jenny's tears got wiped away." Check. "Yes, I kissed Bill on my way in from work as he was leaving for work." Check. "Yes, Andrew got a hug early this morning." Check. "Yes, I took that walk I needed to take." Check.

Our drive toward productive efficiency puts a barrier between us and our mates, between us and our children. We depend upon the impersonal intelligence of our technology to run our lives. Our lives are no longer made by hand, re-created day by day, formed by our needs, wants, and wishes.

> *I have a cell phone, a pager, a fax, and an internet connection with me at all times. I can work anywhere and be found at a moment's notice by my office or clients. I always thought that the better the technology, the more I could accomplish and achieve. Now, I'm more behind than ever. I stiffen each time my pager or cell phone goes off, and my company just sent me to a seminar called, "The New Efficiency: Working Smarter at the Speed of Light!"*
>
> —Benson, fifty

Whose Life Is It, Anyway?

Many of us have forgotten that we have choices in how we live our lives. We look at where we are today and wonder how we got here. "How did I get stuck driving an hour to work and back again each day?" "Why are my teenage daughter and I so estranged?" "How did I suddenly become forty pounds overweight?" "Why don't I ever tend to my garden anymore?" "When did I last write to my favorite cousin?" "How can I be ready for the holidays with so many gifts left to buy?" These and many other questions may take us unawares in quiet moments, perhaps gazing out a window at our weed-choked garden or in the trance of driving down the freeway. Then, we may catch a brief glimpse of what our lives might be if...

If we didn't have this huge house payment, I could spend more time at home.

If I found a job closer to home, I could eat breakfast with my family.

If I stopped smoking, I could use the extra money for new landscaping.

If we started a drop-in center in that old, empty building down the street, our teenagers could have a place to go at night.

If I organized a neighborhood work crew, we could clean up the creek that runs behind our apartments.

If I spent more time with my son, then we could know each other better, and he might not get into so much trouble.

We can use our "what ifs" to keep us unhappily stuck where we are, or we can use them to inspire new ideas, new hope, new ways of doing things. We have the FamilyMind Question as a guide, "What does our family need now, including me?" "What do we REALLY need now, including me?" We may be afraid to ask this hard question because of the hard answers we may find. Maybe our family would be better off if we sold our big, beautiful suburban home and moved to a smaller, cozier, more rural place. What would happen if I quit my job and started my own firm from an office at home? Would our children get a better education if we home-schooled them? Maybe I will put off my career until my children are older. I will give up my job and let my wife pursue her career in another city.

> *I have been the mom-at-home for fifteen years, and I've enjoyed most of it. Just recently I joined a friend in her flower shop. It is a dream come true. Working with the flowers and with customers is a joyous experience, and it's so much fun! The shop is one place where I feel sure of my talents and resources. Then my mother died unexpectedly, and I thought my good luck had ended. Her*

death was such a shock and left me with so many lose ends to complete that I didn't see how I could do it all— take care of Mother's things, comfort and take care of Dad, keep up the meals and the housework at home, and still work in the flower shop. My friend was very understanding and gave me time off, but being away from the shop was like another death. Finally, my husband asked us all to sit down together and talk about what we needed to do to get through this crisis. As I timidly shared my feelings about working in the flower shop, I was amazed at the compassion on the faces of my husband and children. The boys seemed to be seeing the Real Me apart from the My Mother role for the first time. To my surprise, my family took on many of the tasks concerning Mother's things and Dad's needs that I had been trying to do on my own. They also decided to help more at home. Everything is not getting done at home, but we all feel together in making things work, and we've slowed down enough to feel how sad the loss of my mom really is. We now take time to tell stories about her that we want to remember.

—Helen, forty-six

Bringing FamilyMind Home

Like the Hundredth Monkey principle, when enough of us question what we and our families really, really need and begin making choices from those needs, we regain our souls, those lost parts of us that are out there in forgotten dreams, frustrated plans, and trampled hopes. We begin to rebuild the sense of family as a haven to come home to where we are loved for who we truly are. Using FamilyMind thinking comes more naturally to some of us than it does for others. The following suggestions for supporting each other in its use may be helpful.

Be each other's cheerleaders. A favorite teacher of ours believes that two people marry to help each other find God—our soul's deepest desires. Perhaps we do this for our children, as well, or they for us.

> *It is love that reveals to us the eternal in us*
> *and in our neighbors.*[2]

—Miguel de Unamuno, *Tragic Sense of Life*

⊰ *JEANNE* The challenges of marriage and parenting pushed me to re-evaluate my belief system, my motives for doing things. Things like how and why I said "No" to our children. Did I say it because my mother always said "No" to that, because the children's safety was at stake, or because they needed to learn something? I was also forced to look deep inside to discover where I wasn't allowing love in. I had all these deep yearnings inside me that I walled off, because I grew up believing that we never *really* get what we want—our soul's desires. I thought being married and having children would further deprive me of what I really wanted in my life. Because I saw it that way, that was my experience in the beginning. I felt cheated, smothered, and lost until I realized that I was an important member of the family, whose needs and soul desires were precious, too. What helped change my perspective? Don's curiosity about what I thought, how I felt about things, and what I wanted in life. He continually urged me to voice my true feelings. He'd say, "Okay. I know what you *don't* want. Now tell me what you *do* want." By being my cheerleader, Don helped me see that tending to my own needs and desires was not only vital for myself but was an example for our children. Before we can truly give, we have to be full ourselves.

Being each other's cheerleaders allows freedom for our souls, our children's souls, and the souls of our families to grow and bloom. It means we stand on the sidelines and give our whole-hearted support to each other's inner growth. Being emotionally available allows others to bring forth heart-felt questions and longings. Being curious about each other's thoughts, dreams, and needs enables us to get clear about our soul's desires. Sometimes voicing them to a family member who listens without judgment is enough. Sometimes we must rename them, or clarify them, so our loved one gains self-understanding and compassion.

<table>
<tr><td>☙ ☙ DON</td><td>I constantly work on the habit of overcommitting myself. Jeanne recently confronted me about repairing the screen door that I promised to fix several months ago. I felt ashamed, blamed, and left out. Jeanne responded to my defensive, angry retort by saying, "I guess you don't understand how important you are to me." "Huh? I'm important to you?" I said. "Yes!" she responded. "I don't want you to overcommit, fail, and feel bad about yourself. I love you. I want you to be happy about what you agree to do, and I want the screen door fixed!" I never thought of it that way. Milegro pequeño!</td></tr>
</table>

Follow the Four-Fold Way.[3] Angeles Arrien offers four ways to truly participate in life.

1. Show up and choose to be present. This is the first and most important step in creating FamilyMind thinking. Making a conscious choice to be here and to pay attention to the moments we share creates feelings of trust, belonging, and love within a family. This means we are not distracted by reading the newspaper at meals, watching television while children ask about their homework, or doing the laundry immediately after the family returns home from work, school, and so on.

2. Pay attention to what has heart and meaning. How many times have we found ourselves doing what we do not really want to be doing? We pursue a certain career, because our father advised us to. We spend holidays with relatives we do not really enjoy being around. We say "Yes" to church committees, because we think we should. We volunteer for community projects, because it is expected of us. Often we feel overworked, overcommitted, and underappreciated with little

time for ourselves and our families. Where has the joy in our lives gone? When we pay attention to what touches our hearts and gives us meaning and belonging, we find the *joie de vivre* that is our birthright.

3. Tell the truth without blame or judgment. Learning to express our feelings when something is not right or is bothering us without accusing or criticizing the other person involved is an essential family skill. Judgments and accusations only lead to power struggles and misunderstandings. When we begin an expression with "You," or "He," we can be fairly certain of judgment. "You hurt me!" or "She hit me!" we often hear our children say, with little thought to what preceded the hurtful words or actions. When we begin our truth-telling with "I," we are being authentic with our feelings and are more easily heard by another. "I feel angry when you forget to put gas in the car." "I am afraid I will be hurt when you drive so fast." "When you leave your dirty clothes on the bathroom floor, I feel taken for granted." These truthful statements relay our feelings without excessive blame or judgment of another's actions. Now, communication is open for more expression of feelings, apologies, or problem solving.

4. Be open and unattached to outcome. How many times have we failed to recognize a gift, because it did not come in the manner we thought it should?

A small boy looked furtively around him in the Berkeley Rose Garden to see if anyone was watching. Quickly he picked a small rosebud, ran to his mother, and said, "Mommy, you're as beautiful as this rose!" His mother, pleased, replied, "Oh, thank you, Jesse. But why don't you ever tell me you love me?"[4]

—Angeles Arrien,
adapted from a story from *Gathering Medicine*

Being open and unattached to the outcome of events, from our summer vacation to a leisurely walk around the block, frees us to experience the *milagros pequeños*, the epiphanies, the serendipitous moments that spontaneously occur when we truly trust the will of the Divine. This means being able to trust the Divine within ourselves and within our children. Letting go of the need to control our lives releases us to find our heart's desire in all we do.

Strengthen personal boundaries by learning to say "Yes" and "No." Angeles Arrien is fond of saying that English is the only language where "No" means, "I don't love you."[5] We feel guilty when we say "No." We go into long explanations about why. And if the other person pushes us hard enough, we might even change our "No" to "Yes." This happens especially often with our children. Saying "No" is setting an important limit or boundary for our own or another's well-being.

Some of us are afraid of saying "Yes," because it implies we are in agreement with another's ideas or thoughts. "Yes" merely means, "Yes, I see what you mean." Or, "Yes, I want to come to your party." Saying "Yes" also sets limits and boundaries about what we are willing to do. Learning to say "Yes" and "No" when we mean it, is an important component of FamilyMind thinking. Checking inside to know how we feel about a "Yes" or "No" situation and asking, "What does this family need right now, including me?" keeps us out of those tight spots where we are doing something we really do not want to do. Practice saying "Yes" and "No" firmly and kindly without long-winded explanations.

"Oh, I couldn't possibly do that. Thanks, anyway!"

"No, I'm sorry. I'm not taking on anything more."

"Yes, I see your point, but I need it by tonight."

"Yes, I'd love to come. What time?"

Learn to lead *and* to follow. A group of any kind is always in trouble if there are no leaders and only followers, or only leaders and no followers. We say over and over again that children learn best through our examples. We stress this point, because our children learn by watching our behavior *no matter what we do*. When Dad is the Man of the House, makes all the decision, and is always in the leader position, children learn that is what fathers (men) do. When Mom is agreeable, complacent, and always yields to Dad as the leader, children learn that is what mothers (women) do. The other way around is, of course, also true. A family functions best when all members are allowed to express their own ideas and suggestions and to learn cooperation by being *both* a leader and a follower, according to their ages and abilities. By watching Mom and Dad discuss the big and little things, each adding their own thoughts and ideas, children learn the ingredients of healthy family dynamics. Learning to make compromises that include what the family needs and putting these decisions into action for the benefit of all, requires that everyone take turns at leading and following.

Leading may be as simple as a child choosing what bedtime story to read. With practice we learn what a good leader does and what *style* of leadership is most effective. If, for example, our son leads like a dictator and deliberately chooses a bedtime story that everyone hates, he has to suffer the resistance he encounters, like Don did on our Mexican vacation described in an earlier chapter. He learns that the most effective leader takes his followers' needs and preferences, as well as his own, into account when making his decisions.

Following can be just as hard as leading for some of us. Having to have our own way, needing to be right, and thinking we have all the answers makes following very difficult. To Henry, yielding to the needs of the family, meant always having to give up what he wanted.

Until I learned that asking what the family needs included my needs, too, I was a very hard leader to follow and a very uncooperative follower. My wife and kids were either in tears or sullen and cowed. I ran into trouble at work, too. If I gave in to what the group wanted, I'd end up doing something I hated, like going with the family to an amusement park, or getting stuck with the financial end of a project. Then I discovered that as both a leader and a follower, my needs could be considered, too. I didn't always have to

*give in to something I don't enjoy doing. I could have
my joys, too.*

—Henry, thirty-three

Practice giving *and* receiving. Giving and receiving are like leading
and following; the opinions, desires, and preferences of others, as
well as our own, must be considered. Mistakes happen when we give
to others the way we like being given to *without considering whether
they like things that way, too.* When we look *only* through our own
lenses of likes and dislikes and give what *we* want them to have, we
often miss the other person, or the group, entirely. Does this situation sound familiar?

> ❧ *JEANNE* | For Christmas one year, Don gave me a lovely pair of silk
> pajamas. But, they were dark blue. I love blue on other peo-
> ple, and Don looks terrific in blue. I, however, take on an
> awful shade of yellow when I wear dark blue, so I don't. I was
> touched by the expensive gift, but I felt hurt that after ten
> years, Don didn't know this about me.

Experiences are similar on the receiving end of things. When we
expect to receive things in a certain way, because of how our family
of origin gave and received, or just because we want things that way,
we often miss the intended gift or caring.

> ❧ ❧ *DON* | One Father's Day I pictured sleeping late, breakfast in bed, a
> pile of gifts, and lots of hugs from family. I didn't make a big
> deal out of any of this, but when the day didn't go as I had
> planned, I started feeling un-cared for. Jeanne and my son
> were trying hard, but when I told them what I wanted, they
> had a private discussion, and asked me if we could start the
> day again. This time, they asked me what I wanted and took
> care to give in a way I could receive. I, in turn, paid more
> attention to the care they gave me. It turned out to be one of
> the best Father's Days I've ever had.

**For men only: DO NOT flaunt your FamilyMind thinking
abilities.** An unhappy tendency for some of us is to think we have it,

get too sure of ourselves, start bragging in groups with friends, and start instructing others, as though we were the one who discovered this great way of being in a family. Women hate this. First of all, many women may be suspicious of this new behavior. They think, "Oh, sure. He's promised to change before. It lasted for a few weeks, and then he forgot all about it." They remember the hope before and the letdown afterward.

> *My husband was all excited about FamilyMind thinking. I thought, "I'll believe it when I see it." That's when he surprised me by helping me carry in the groceries and putting the food away—pretty much in the customary places. Then he made lunch—for all of us! This was great, and he was really pleased with himself. The kids even noticed he made lunch for everyone, rather than just for himself, like in the past. That's when I got my hopes up. Then, Sonny fell down, bumping his head on the corner of the coffee table, Sara started screaming at the sight of blood, and the phone rang. My husband, Jack, yells that he's expecting a call from work and runs to answer it, leaving me with two, small, out-of-control children to soothe and nurse. "So much for asking what this family needs right now," I thought, and I felt truly betrayed and sad.*
>
> —*Nicole, thirty-seven*

Old habits are hard to break. Just when we think we have the hang of it, we slip up and forget, or get angry and retreat. This is the natural way of things. We go in and out of FamilyMind thinking all the time! The best way to recover after a slip is to admit we goofed, forgive ourselves, ask others for forgiveness, and carry on. Remember that learning something new takes time, and each step provides opportunities for connecting with other family members and for learning more about them and about ourselves.

For women only: Allow for different ways of doing things. Does this sound familiar? "My wife asks me to do something, so I do it.

Then she turns around and does it over, because I didn't do it *her* way." Most mothers are so busy that any help around the house, no matter how it is done, is life-saving. For some of us, however, sharing our power at home feels like giving up something precious, and we are afraid of the loss. Having clean sheets folded just so and lined up in the linen closet, filling the dishwasher in a way that gets every last dirty dish, and arranging the painting supplies for an easy cleanup when Junior is finished, give many of us a feeling of contentment.

> ⇨ JEANNE | I feel safe when I know that I can always go to the cupboard to the right of the stove and find the bundt pan on the middle shelf. And this may sound silly, but it gives me great satisfaction to see the clean towels folded and neatly stacked in their closet. When the house is a mess, I feel messy on the inside.

For some women, it is an issue of safety. For others, it is an issue of power. Catherine, a mother at one of our workshops, says that her mother was in charge of the house. "It was her domain, no ifs, ands, or buts about it. And my father never tried to interfere. Even if he had wanted to help, my mother would never have allowed it. Having grown up with this model, I have trouble sharing the power with my husband. I like things a certain way, and he just can't seem to do it. I'd rather do it myself than to try to train him. Besides, I like being in control at home."

Many of us in our heart of hearts feel as Catherine does. However, our workloads, both inside and outside the house, are so great that we must accept help. We cannot do it all, and our mates will do things differently, from changing the baby's diaper to watering the lawn. We can count on it, but it helps to remember that *different does not mean wrong*. Besides, sharing the big and little tasks with a partner can be less stressful, gratifying, and more enjoyable than doing it all alone.

Avoid performance ratings. There is nothing worse than having our mate tell us we failed when we are learning something new. It is easy to gloat and judge when one of us fails in our endeavors to use FamilyMind thinking. We may be too quick to fling at our spouse, "See, I knew you couldn't think about the family group! You're so focused on your job, that we don't exist."

Remembering that we *will* go in and out of FamilyMind thinking and that our performance will never be absolutely perfect enables us to feel compassion and empathy for the other's efforts, rather than ridicule and judgment. Just as soon as we judge others for their actions, we slip up and react in a narcissistic way, leaving ourselves open to a critical performance rating. FamilyMind thinking flourishes best in an atmosphere of kindness, acceptance of human weakness, forgiveness, and love.

Know the "holes in the sidewalk."[6] We all have them—these sides of our natures that trap us into bothersome behaviors we vowed never to do again, because they leave us feeling left out and unloved. Maybe we get angry too fast, or launch into a lecture or sermon too readily. Perhaps we are too quick to judge, use sarcasm or shame to get our way, think only of ourselves, or think only of others. These are behaviors we employ to protect ourselves when life gets tense, uncomfortable, and overwhelming. Habitual use of these behaviors makes relationships with others difficult, ending in power struggles, hurt feelings, resentment, and mutiny. These are the holes we fall into when things get rough. Identifying these old behaviors helps us recognize them *before* we repeat them. Then we can say, "Oops, there I go again. That's old stuff and no longer fits. This is what I would rather say or do."

In a Nutshell

We believe that FamilyMind thinking offers a lifeline to all of us who struggle in our families. It is a lifelong process to share and expand upon. The FamilyMind Question, "What do we need right now, including me?" is adaptable to any family configuration or circumstance, and we offer it as a seed to be planted, nurtured, and grown into a way of thinking that makes our families work according to our own needs and definitions. FamilyMind is all of the following and much more:

- building relationships through daily rhythms
- doing what is needed

- knowing what we need
- discovering what others need
- re-evaluating our assumptions regularly
- understanding ourselves and others
- working together to help everyone get what they need
- finding what works, no matter how unusual the solution
- giving and receiving according to our abilities
- sharing feelings
- looking for compromises
- supporting others

Living on Planet Parenthood with FamilyMind is a process always in flux. The goal is neither *progress* nor *perfection*. Rudolf Steiner believed that children did not need perfect parents; rather, they needed parents who were continually striving to be better.[7] To give ourselves feedback about how FamilyMind is working for us, we must ask:

- Is it working?
- Am I striving?
- Am I feeling better?
- Are my family relationships better?
- Am I developing in ways that are satisfying to me?
- Am I contributing to my family and my community?
- Am I living a handmade life, shaping it with my own hands day by day, according to what I need, want, and wish for?

Raising a family is too big and too precious a task to do all alone. Ask for help and explain FamilyMind to partners, other family members, grandparents, neighbors, friends, teachers, co-workers, day care staff,

and anyone you meet. We invite you to send us your experiences—
what works and what does not work—so we can all learn together
how better to raise our families.

Endnotes: Part Twelve

1. Ken Keyes, Jr., *The Hundredth Monkey* (St. Mary, KT: Vision Books, 1981), 19.

2. Miguel de Unamuno, *Tragic Sense of Life* (New York: Dover, 1954).

3. Angeles Arrien, *The Four-Fold Way* (San Francisco: Harper San Francisco, 1993).

4. Angeles Arrien, *Gathering Medicine: Stories, Songs, and Methods for Soul Retrieval*, audiocassette produced by Sounds True Recording, Boulder, CO, 1994, Part One.

5. Arrien, *The Four-Fold Way*.

6. Portia Nelson, *There's a Hole in My Sidewalk* (Hillsboro, OR: Beyond Words, 1993).

7. Rahima Baldwin, *You Are Your Child's First Teacher* (Berkeley, CA: Celestial Arts, 1989).

Index